german

language
life
& culture

IAN ROBERTS

TEACH YOURSELF BOOKS

For Emily Kate – born 11th October 1999

For UK orders: please contact Bookpoint Ltd, 39 Milton Park, Abingdon, Oxon OX14 4TD. Telephone: (44) 01235 400414, Fax: (44) 01235 400454. Lines are open from 9.00–6.00, Monday to Saturday, with a 24 hour message answering service. Email address: orders@bookpoint.co.uk

For USA. & Canada orders: please contact NTC/Contemporary Publishing, 4255 West Touhy Avenue, Lincolnwood, Illinois 60646–1975, USA. Telephone: (847) 679 5500, Fax: (847) 679 2494.

Long renowned as the authoritative source for self-guided learning – with more than 30 million copies sold worldwide – the *Teach Yourself* series includes over 200 titles in the fields of languages, crafts, hobbies, business and education.

A catalogue entry for this title is available from The British Library.

Library of Congress Catalog Card Number: On file

First published in UK 2000 by Hodder Headline Plc, 338 Euston Road, London, NW1 3BH.

First published in US 2000 by NTC/Contemporary Publishing, 4255 West Touhy Avenue, Lincolnwood (Chicago), Illinois 60646–1975 USA.

The 'Teach Yourself' name and logo are registered trade marks of Hodder & Stoughton Ltd.

Copyright © 2000   Ian Roberts

Typeset by Transet Limited, Coventry, England.
Printed in Great Britain for Hodder & Stoughton Educational, a division of Hodder Headline Plc, 338 Euston Road, London NW1 3BH by Cox & Wyman Ltd, Reading, Berkshire.

Impression number   10 9 8 7 6 5 4 3 2
Year   2005 2004 2003 2002 2001 2000

CONTENTS

INTRODUCTION

This book is designed to give you as full a basic overview as possible of the main aspects of Germany: the country, its languages, its people, their way of life and culture and wat makes them tick.

You will find it a useful foundation if you are studying for examinations which require a knowledge of the background of Germany and its civilization, or if you are learning the language in, for example, an evening class and want to know more about the country and how it works. If your job inolves travel and business relations it will provide valuable and practical information about the ways and customs of the people you are working with. Or if you simply have an interest in Germany for whatever reason, it will broaden your knowledge about the country and its inhabitants.

The book is divided into three sections:

■ **The making of Germany**

Chapters One and Two deal with the forces – historical, geographical, geological, demographical and linguistic – that have brought about the formation of the country we know as Germany and the language we know as German. Chapter Two also takes a look at the role of German outside the immediate frontiers of Germany.

■ **Creative Germany**

Chapters three to Seven deal with the wealth of creative aspects of German culture from the beginning to the present day. These chapters take a look at the main areas or works of literature, art and architecture, music, traditions and festivals, science and technology, fashion and food and drink, together with the people who have created and are still creating them.

■ Living in Germany now

Chapters Eight to Eleven deal with aspects of contemporary German society and the practicalities of living in present-day Germany: the way the political structure of the country is organized, education, the environment, the workplace and how people spend their leisure time. The final chapter looks at the country's political, economic and social relations with the wider world, and takes a glance at the future.

Taking it further

Each chapter ends with a section entitled 'Taking it further', where you will find useful addresses, websites, suggested places to visit and things to see and do in order to develop your interest further and increase your knowledge.

The language

Within each chapter you will encounter a number of terms in German, whose meaning is given in English when they are first introduced. If you wish to put your knowledge into practice, we have provided in each chapter a list of useful words and phrases to enable you to talk or write about the subject in question.

We have been careful in researching and checking facts, but please be aware that sources sometimes offer differing information. Of course a book of this length cannot contain everything you may need to know on every aspect of Germany. That is why we have provided so many pointers to where you can find further information about any aspect that you may wish to pursue in more depth. We trust that you will enjoy this introductory book, and that it will provide leads to further profitable reading, listening and visiting.

Gute Reise!

Phil Turk
Series Editor

AUTHOR'S NOTE

As astonishing as it may seem to older readers, a whole generation of Germans has already grown up with no awareness of what it was like in Germany before the fall of the Iron Curtain in that amazing summer and autumn of 1989. Even though these events occurred a little over ten years ago, the fact remains that, historically speaking, the forty-year period when Germany was divided will increasingly be viewed merely as an historical blip in the process of Unification: The Holy Roman Empire, Bismarck's Prussian-dominated Second Reich, Hitler's attempts to create a *Großdeutschland*, and finally post-Wall Germany at the heart of a Europe which is itself seemingly on course for political union.

In this study, therefore, I have chosen to view events in East Germany between 1945 and 1989/1990 purely from a contemporary (West) German perspective, with apologies to those who – rightly – consider themselves to be East Germans first and foremost. This is not to say that I have dismissed the Socialist Germany out of hand. You will see, as you read through the book, that specific aspects of that state have been singled out for particular attention at the appropriate moment. Nevertheless, I feel sure that history will, ultimately, ensure that it is the days and weeks leading up to Unification, and the months and years afterwards, which are of the most interest to the student of contemporary German life, language and culture.

Ian Roberts

1 | THE MAKING OF GERMANY

Lying as it does in the heart of modern-day Europe, Germany has always played a central role in the history and politics of the continent. Indeed, on many occasions the impact of Germany's actions have spread right around the world. Certainly most people are familiar with the historical Germany which plunged the globe into two world wars. Many also mention the country's economic strength today: indeed, the German people are rightly proud of the effect that the words 'Made in Germany' now have. But there is a lot more to the land, and its people, than that.

Geography

The country we now call Germany enjoys a central position in Western Europe, bordered by no fewer than nine countries: Denmark to the north, Poland and the Czech Republic to the east, Austria and Switzerland to the south, and France and the Benelux countries of Belgium, the Netherlands and Luxembourg to the west. The country is some 1000km long at its longest point from north to south, and 600km wide. Not surprisingly, therefore, the physical appearance of the country changes greatly as you travel through it.

The northern coast

In the North the landscape is dominated by flat arable land being grazed by black and white Frisian cows (which originally came from this area). On the coasts, the **Wattland** is a region of mudflats which can extend out to sea for miles during low tide. Horse-drawn wagons and hikers, called **Wattwanderer**, make their way at low

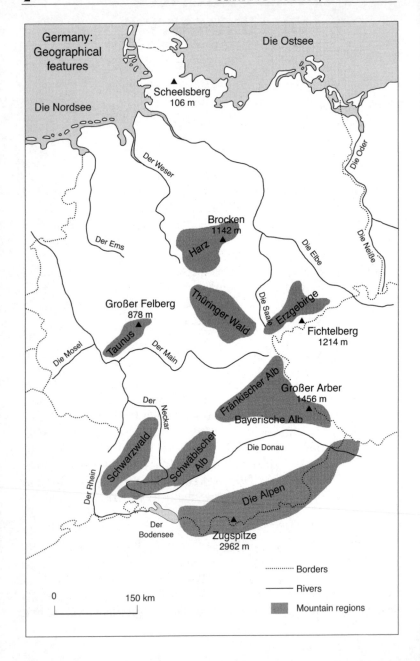

Germany: Geographical features

tide to the curious little islands which poke up out of the sea of mud. The houses on these islands, and along much of the North German coast, are sturdy little brick affairs, their whitewashed walls and red tiled roofs standing out like the many lighthouses which are also dotted along the coast. Further east, the German **Ostseeküste** (Baltic coast) boasts some wonderful beaches, and the spectacular rugged coastal cliffs of Rügen.

Mid-Germany

Generally, as you move south, past the major northern cities of Hamburg, Bremen and Rostock, the average height of the country above sea level slowly rises. The heathland of **Niedersachsen** (Lower Saxony) and the sandy moorland of the **Mark Brandenburg** (Brandenburg Marches) around Berlin gradually give way to higher regions. In a broad belt running from west to east across the country, other small hill and mountain ranges speak of greater things to come: the Eifel on the French border; the low hills of the Taunus, whose warm, south-facing slopes support a long-established wine-growing industry; the Harz mountains, which rise to a height of 1142m; and the **Erzgebirge** (Ore Mountains), also reaching over 1000m, which form the border between that part of Germany and the Czech Republic.

The south and the Alps

Further south again, as we reach southern Germany proper, two things are noticed in particular. First, the landscape is increasingly characterised by huge tracts of forest. This is not to say that there are no trees further north (indeed, one of the main impressions of a journey through Germany is of endless woods and forests), but now we begin to see the outlying areas of the truly vast forests of Bavaria and, most famous of all, the south-western **Schwarzwald** (Black Forest), of gateau and cuckoo clock fame! The second aspect of this landscape is a slow awareness of the land climbing and climbing. As you pass Stuttgart, into the Schwäbische Alp, and continue towards the **Bodensee** (Lake Constance) and the Swiss border; or when you reach the area of München (Munich), the first foothills of the Alps, the **Voralpen**, begin to rise before you. Here in the Alps we find the Zugspitze, Germany's highest, truly alpine mountain at 2963m above sea level.

Climate

Not surprisingly, Germany's climate varies hugely too. In the north a maritime climate prevails, with mild winters and breezy summers, but as we move south and east so the climate comes to be dominated by Germany's continental position: cold, snowy winters give way to almost unbearably hot summers. In the extreme south, the Alps play their own part, providing a paradise for lovers of winter sports. They are responsible, too, for the remarkable climatic phenomenon known as the **Föhn**, a warm wind which blows down from the mountains onto the lower plains of **Bayern** (Bavaria) and **Schwaben** (Swabia), creating an intensely clear quality to the air which brings far-off objects startlingly close. **Föhn** makes Munich appear to be nestling right underneath the Alps, even though they are still some 90km away. It is also blamed for bad headaches and bad tempers, not to mention an increase in road accidents!

Germany: A country of rivers

Germany is also a country of rivers. In the north the wide Elbe allowed Hamburg to grow into a wealthy and important sea trading centre in late medieval times. This river begins its journey hundreds of kilometres away in Dresden, in the east. There we find the two rivers which formed the post-war border between what was then the **Deutsche Demokratische Republik** (German Democratic Republic, or East Germany) and Poland: the Rivers Oder and Neiße. In the south the **Donau** (Danube) begins its long journey west of Freiburg, and travels eastwards past Augsburg and Regensburg before crossing into Austria and on towards Hungary.

Of all the many German rivers (we haven't even mentioned the Main, where the financial capital of Frankfurt grew up; the Spree, Berlin's main waterway; or the Neckar, where the first 'Germans' settled in the Stone Age), by far and away the most important is, of course, the Rhine. **Der Rhein**, as the Germans call it, is an amazing stretch of water. Its source lies in the **Schwarzwald**, north east of Freiburg, and passes through, or near, the important centres of Stuttgart, Heidelberg, Mainz, Köln (Cologne), Bonn and Düsseldorf before crossing into the Netherlands and eventually reaching the North Sea, some 1300km after its journey began. The

Rhein not only formed an important trade route from the earliest days of Germany's history, but it is also provides some of the country's most romantic scenery, with medieval castles perched on high cliffs above picturesque towns and villages clinging to the narrow shore of the great river. It is no surprise that the **Rheintal** (Rhine valley) is one of the most popular tourist regions in Germany.

The origins of Germany

■ Germanic tribes and the decline of Rome
■ The empire of the Franks

Watching over the barbarians.

The English name of Germany has its origins in the idea of 'all coming from the same roots'. In fact, there was a massive number of tribes and peoples which fed into the modern-day Germans, and many of their names are still familiar today: **Franken**, **Gothen**, **Hunnen**, **Vandalen** and **Sachsen**, to name a few. The Romans regarded the German barbarian tribes as a wild race that could not be conquered, merely contained. They built a defensive line, known as the *limes* (pronounced 'leems'), from the Rhine at Koblenz for hundreds of kilometres to Regensburg on the Danube. Despite watch towers and garrison forts, the *pax romana* in these border lands was very fragile, and as the might of Rome faded, so the Germanic tribes spread. The barbarians entered Roman territory and gradually mingled with the existing Romanised

German nations. Over the centuries certain groups grew to dominate their areas: the Frisians in the north, the Saxons in the east, the Bavarians in the south, the Alemanns in the Rhein-Neckar basin, the Franks to the west (including large parts of modern France) and the Thuringians in the centre and east. Eventually, the Franks became the most powerful, and for several hundred years in the 5th to 8th centuries their royal dynasties exercised a limited form of power over the neighbouring regions.

Charlemagne

It was under Karl der Große (died 814, Karl the Great is more usually known as Charlemagne) that something like a German nation began to emerge. Upon gaining the throne of the Frankish lands he quickly occupied his neighbours' lands, and in 800 was crowned first **Römischer Kaiser** (Roman Emperor) of the Germans. This empire stretched from northern Germany, to large parts of France in the west and Hungary in the east, and all the way down to Rome itself. In the following centuries Karl's successors, such as Otto I (912–973; coronation in 936), tried to maintain control of this collection of states, but could not create a single, unified country.

Medieval Germany

■ The German dynasties
■ Friedrich 'Barbarossa'

After the Frankish monarchs, a number of families established dynasties which would, in turn, set the tone for the country's development for hundreds of years: names such as the Welfs of Saxony, the Bavarian Wittelsbachs and the Hohenstaufen dynasty of Swabia. Some of the dynasties' kings, such as the Hohenstaufen king Friedrich I, the 'Barbarossa' (Redbeard), have gone down in history. He ruled from 1152 until his death in 1197, and earned a reputation as a tough leader. This was a period when strong warrior kings held court over a strict feudal system, while the princes and knights under their patronage squabbled among themselves. Occasionally they would settle their differences and fight the heathen Moors together in the Crusades, but generally they looked after their own interests first.

Kingdom of Denmark

Pomerania

Saxony

East March

POLAND

(Eastern territories still disputed)

(Upper)

Aachen ●

Lorraine

Thuringia

Franconia

Bohemia

Moravia

(Lower)

FRANCE
(formerly East Frankish kingdom)

Swabia

Bavaria

Bavarian East Mark

HUNGARY

● Munich

Kingdom of Burgundy

Steiermark

Carinthia

Kingdom of Italy

Venice

Croatia

Rome ●

The German Empire in the 11th and 12th Centuries

●●●●●●●● Boundary of the empire

--------- State boundaries

■ Expansion eastwards and the foundation of Prussia
■ The Plague and early anti-Jewish feeling
■ The rise of the towns

At the same time, this young nation began to expand eastwards. In 1226 a group of German nobles calling themselves the Knights of the Teutonic Order founded the nation of **Preußen** (Prussia) in the East. They fought over these marcher lands with the Poles for some 200 years. During this period, too, the Plague was to have a particular effect on German society. Paranoia in the towns meant that the **Juden** – communities of Jews who had fled persecution in other countries – were quickly treated as scapegoats. In **Nürnberg** (Nuremberg) in 1349, a single pogrom resulted in the burning at the stake of more than 500 Jews. These two factors – the **Drang nach Osten** (the urge to spread to the east) and suspicion of the Jews – would haunt Germany's development in the centuries to come.

The final important development in the Middle Ages in Germany was the gradual rise of the towns. As they grew in size and wealth their **Bürger** (citizens) wanted more and more freedom from imperial interference. They formed alliances to resist the power of the princes in the region (e.g. the **Rheinischer Bund**, or Rhine League, founded in 1254), or to ensure favourable trading conditions, easily the most successful being the **Hanseatischer Bund** (1358), the large Hanseatic League of German, English, Danish and other cities on the North Sea and Baltic coasts. (Even today, German cities which belonged to this league, such as Bremen, carry an H prefix to their car number plates, indicating that it is a **Hansastadt**). Sometimes there were brief, and brutal, wars between the different factions and imperial troops. But life, on the whole, steadily improved for the majority of Germany's citizens.

The Holy Roman Empire of the German nation

Martin Luther and the Reformation

By the start of the 16th century the states of Germany were nominally united, under the rule of the emperor Maximilian I (crowned 1493), and known together as **das Heilige Römische Reich Deutscher Nation** – the Holy Roman Empire of the German Nation. The reality of this grand title, however, was that Germany was made up of a complex pattern of separate territories, towns and nation states, which owed their allegiance to the Emperor, or to the church, or to no one at all. All of this guaranteed a great deal of upheaval in the next 200 years or so.

One crucial event in the process was started by the Augustinan monk Martin Luther in 1517. Sickened by the corruption of the Church and the Pope, he nailed 95 **Thesen** – points of complaint and debate – to the doors of the church in Wittenberg, calling for a reform of religious practice. Thanks to the protests of this one man, the movement which came to be known as the Reformation, and the protesting (or Protestant) church, was born.

Social unrest: the *Bauernkriege*

Luther's ideas, and those of many others who quickly added their voices to the debate, fuelled a burning desire for social and religious reform. In 1524 the peasants revolted in the **Bauernkriege** (Peasants' war). Seeing their opportunity, many regional princes turned to Protestantism and led the peasants. The 'war' – really a series of regional clashes – lasted only two years, and saw more than 100,000 peasants killed in brutal reprisals. But by the end, the two factions of Catholic and Protestant (often supported by men with political, rather than religious motives) were more deeply divided than ever. For nearly 100 years the fortunes of the Protestants varied.

The Thirty Years' War

■ Defenestration of Prague
■ Civil War

In May 1618 a group of Protestants travelled to Prague (at this time the capital of German Bohemia) to complain about their poor treatment when compared with their Catholic fellows. When their complaints were rejected, the angry nobles threw two Catholic court officials out of an upstairs window (this is what the word 'defenestration' actually means). Although the two men landed on a pile of manure, unharmed, the Protestant group now had no chance of having their complaints heard. Within a short time civil war was raging between the Emperor's Catholic troops and the forces of the Protestant princes and towns, right across the country, with the Emperor gaining the upper hand. By the late 1620s the Emperor had taken control of huge parts of Germany. This alarmed the Protestants, of course, but it alarmed many Catholic princes even more, who saw the Emperor growing more and more powerful by the day. A war which had begun over religion quickly became more political in its complexion. Appeals to foreign powers, friendly to one side or the other, saw armies from Sweden, Denmark, France, Spain and the Netherlands marching into German territory.

By the time the Emperor had settled with his princes at the **Prager Frieden** (The Peace of Prague) in 1635, the foreign armies could not be stopped. They ravaged Germany for another 13 years, with fighting raging back and forth across the country, killing as many as one in three of the German population in some areas. Eventually, the **Westfälischer Frieden** (Peace of Westphalia) was signed in 1648, but under the terms of the treaty Sweden retained parts of northern Germany, France gained Alsace, and the Netherlands and Switzerland were excluded from the German empire. Although everyone now accepted that religion should be kept totally apart from matters of state, Germany was even more fragmented than ever before.

The age of absolutism

■ The Enlightenment
■ Germany, land of poet and thinker
■ The Seven Years' War

Some good did come out of the chaos of the 17th century, as individual states began a programme of modest but significant political and social reforms. Although there was little question of the rulers of the states giving up their positions, freedom of thought came to be tolerated in the period known as the **Aufklärung** (Enlightenment). Throughout the following 100 years some of Germany's greatest poets and thinkers were at work in their own states and regions: Kant and Hegel contributed to the Europe-wide philosophical debates; Goethe, Schiller and Herder published literature which many still regard as the best in the German language; and Bach, Haydn and Mozart wrote truly magnificent works of music.

But this period also saw the emergence of Prussia as a major German nation. Under Friedrich I, then Friedrich Wilhelm I, and finally Friedrich II (known as Friedrich der Große), Prussia became a highly organised bureaucratic state, with a well-trained professional army and a large reserve of troops, thanks to an advanced system of limited military service. In 1740, Friedrich der Große invaded Silesia and stole territory from the Austrian Habsburgs, the largest German dynasty at the time. Despite facing the allied might of Austria, France and Russia during the Seven Years' War of 1756–1764, Prussia was firmly established as a serious contender to dominate Germany, and a real political power in Europe.

Revolution!

■ The first French Republic
■ Confederation of the Rhine
■ The end of the Holy Roman Empire

The next major event to shape Germany's destiny was one which touched every single European country. The French Revolution of 1789 did not affect Germany at first. But three years later Napoleon's troops invaded, and there was very little that the German states could do to stop them. Within two years all German lands to the west of the Rhine were in French hands. Sixteen German states chose to leave the German Empire in favour of Napoleon's newly created **Rheinbund**, or Confederation of the Rhine. Among the 16 were such important states as Bavaria, Württemberg and Baden. Their loss was a blow from which the Empire could not recover, and on 6 August 1806 the **Kaiser**, Emperor Franz II, dissolved the Holy Roman Empire.

The rise of Prussia

■ Wars of liberation and defeat for Napoleon
■ Congress of Vienna
■ The **Deutscher Bund**

Until this point Prussia had managed to remain neutral, but declared war on France on 9 October 1806. Events moved with incredible speed: Napoleon's troops smashed the Prussian army at the Battles of Jena and Auerstadt on 14 October, and the **Empereur** held a victory parade in Berlin on 27 October. For several years Prussia was virtually a puppet state until, in the **Befreiungskriege** (wars of liberation), the people discovered a sense of national unity for perhaps the very first time and rose up against the occupying power. Now allied with the other European nations facing Napoleon, Prussia finally defeated the French at the battle of Leipzig, the **Völkerschlacht** (peoples' battle), on 16 October 1813.

The Congress of Vienna, called after France's defeat, created a **Deutscher Bund** (German League, or Confederation) of 34 states and four cities to act as a buffer to any renewed French expansion. Austria and Prussia were easily the largest of the states in the Federation. A parliament, known as the **Bundestag**, was convened in Frankfurt, with each state sending representatives as required. Although Prussia lost some of its eastern territories to Russian Poland, it was granted the regions of the Rhineland and Westphalia, giving it a much larger population. Along with the people came a commodity which was to stand Prussia in very good stead at the beginning of the Industrial Revolution: coal.

The Industrial era

■ The Restoration
■ A growing sense of nationalism

The period immediately after the Congress of Vienna has come to be known as the Restoration, or, in German, the **Vormärz** (literally: pre-March). Many of the reforms introduced in response to Napoleon's successes were revoked: liberal organisations (especially the Socialists and reform-minded groups in the universities) were banned, and leading democrats were jailed. Strict censorship was introduced and the education system was brought under tight state control. It seemed as if democracy had taken a major step backwards.

But the process of democracy was not dead. The first signs of the Industrial Revolution, which arrived late to Germany, were creating a new social group: the workers. Although they were not yet organised, or even particularly aware of the political situation, workers' grumblings of discontent early in the 19th century were growing louder. At the same time, writers such as the Grimm brothers (who recorded the oral tradition of German folk tales) and Georg Büchner were making the German people aware, perhaps for the first time, of their common heritage. An intellectual by the name of Karl Marx was also writing down his ideas for a more just society. In 1832 some 30,000 people gathered for a festival at Hambach under the liberal, revolutionary colours of **schwarz–rot–gold** (black–red–gold), calling for a free, united Germany.

The pace of change began to pick up. The **Deutscher Zollverein** (German Trade Organisation; **Zoll** = customs) was founded in 1834 by a coalition of 18 German states, guaranteeing favourable trade conditions among members. Austria declined to participate, thinking itself strong enough to operate independently of this new organisation. But as the trade in coal, steel and other commodities vital for the growing factories and heavy industries flourished, so the Prussian **Thaler** became the common currency throughout Germany. Prussia was now one of the strongest states in Europe.

1848 and the Frankfurt Parliament

■ New revolutions in Europe
■ The short-lived **Nationalversammlung**

The 1800s saw discontent growing: the **Bundestag**, the main parliamentary body in Germany, did little more than rubber-stamp the policies of Austria and Prussia. A fresh wave of unrest was triggered off by the second French Revolution in 1848. Even Berlin, capital of the mighty Prussia, was affected, and only brought to order when the king, Friedrich Wilhelm IV, rode through the city dressed in black, red and gold. Later in the day he issued a proclamation that 'from this day Prussia shall merge into Germany'. Out of the chaos a new parliament was elected, the **Nationalversammlung** (National Assembly), which met for the first time in the Paulskirche, Frankfurt, on 18 May 1848. At first there was genuine enthusiasm for this national body. The parliament issued a doctrine of fundamental human rights on 28 December, and on 29 April the following year announced universal male suffrage in all elections. What the parliament lacked, however, was the support of Prussia and Austria. By June 1849 the experiment in democracy was over. Control of the German states returned to the **Bundestag** and the struggle for supremacy between the two main powers continued.

Bismarck and a united Germany

Prussia's struggle with Austria

The ongoing century saw the pace of economic growth accelerate, with Prussia enjoying the best of it. Austria, however, was stuck with a stagnant, agrarian economy and was using precious finances against Russia in the Crimean War in the 1850s. Otto von Bismarck, the Prussian **Ministerpräsident** who had represented his state at the ill-fated Frankfurt parliament, set about preparing his army for war. Cleverly, he remained neutral during the Crimean War, but lent political support to Russia, which angered Austria greatly. But Austria needed Prussia now, as well as new lands to fund its economy. In 1864 the two states invaded the then-Danish territory of Schleswig and Holstein, with a view to sharing its wealth and its administration. But Bismarck, the **Eiserner Kanzler** (Iron Chancellor), had no intention of sharing Prussia's new acquisitions with Austria, or anyone else for that matter. In 1866 he engineered a dispute over Schleswig-Holstein. The Austrian army was easily defeated in a brief battle at Königgrätz and Prussia gained not only the northern states, but also Hanover, Hesse-Kassel, Frankfurt and Nassau.

■ The Franco-Prussian War
■ A second German empire, a united Germany

Next, Bismarck set Prussia on a path to war with France. Again he used a diplomatic trick, this time over the now-vacant Spanish throne, to antagonise the French. France declared war on Prussia on 19 July 1870. The Franco-Prussian War was only ever going to have one outcome, as the French foundered against a Prussian war machine which was now, technologically, vastly superior to any other force in Europe. Seeing Prussia's success, the southern states which had initially lined themselves with Austria against the **Norddeutscher Bund** (Northern German Confederation) now rushed to join it. Their motives were probably a mix of nationalistic fervour and realistic appraisal of where true power lay.

After generations of rivalry Prussia had finally sidelined the Austrian Habsburgs, ensuring that they never again played a role in German politics. (Significantly, it is from this point onwards that we need to view Austria as an entirely separate, non-German country, even if the process of her isolation had been a long one. It also forms the historical basis for Hitler's **Anschluß** (annexation) of Austria in 1938.) On 18 January 1871, in the Hall of Mirrors at Versailles, the Prussian king Wilhelm I proclaimed the new **Deutsches Reich** (German empire). Although some were disappointed at the exclusion of Austria, and thus the dream of a united **Großdeutschland** (Greater Germany), the fact that Prussia had finally united the German states was enthusiastically applauded.

Otto von Bismarck, Germany's Iron Chancellor and architect of the 1871 Unification.

■ The **Gründerzeit**
■ Gunboat diplomacy and the **Platz an der Sonne**

After the founding of the new **Reich**, in the period known as the **Gründerzeit** (Founding Era), Germany held a very powerful position within European politics. But unlike Britain and France, the other large powers at the time, Germany had no colonies beyond her own shores. With an economy and industry which was still expanding at a fantastic rate, Germany needed such markets to sell her manufactured goods in, and the raw materials which places like Africa offered. The Germans wanted their own **Platz an der Sonne** (place in the sun), and fought hard to establish colonies in southwest and east Africa, as well as in places like Togo and the Solomon Islands. Ironically, the colonies cost Germany far more money and effort than they brought in, and wasted military resources which all too soon would be needed in Europe.

The military state
■ Kaiser Wilhelm
■ Mobilisation for war

In 1890 Wilhelm II succeeded his father, Friedrich III as **Kaiser**. One of his first acts was to move against the powerful Bismarck, who resigned on 18 March 1890. Germany now found herself plagued by a series of rather weak **Kanzler** (chancellors) at a time when fears of the triple entente between France, Russia and Britain were dominating the government's political view. By now the German military had freed itself of all parliamentary restraints, and a massive programme of militarisation was begun to challenge Britain's natural domination of the seas. The **Kaiser** was an enthusiastic supporter of all these nationalistic movements and he and his military chiefs prepared for war.

Assassination in Sarajevo

On 28 June 1914 the Archduke Franz Ferdinand, heir to the Austrian throne, was assassinated by a bomb thrown into his car during a drive through Sarajevo. Austria, which had strategic interests in the region, protested to Serbia and made quite unreasonable demands which the Serbs were unable to meet. Russia mobilised her troops, ready to prevent any Austrian military action. At this time, Austria and Germany were still linked by a mutual defence alliance, signed in 1879. Germany reassured Austria of her intention to honour the pledge – the fact that Austria was committing her ally to a war of aggression was readily overlooked by a nation caught in the grip of **Hurrahpatriotismus**. As Germany mobilised her own formidable forces, women and children lined the streets, cheering enthusiastically. In terms echoed soon after in Britain, people confidently predicted that the impending war would be over before the leaves turned brown in autumn.

The Schlieffen Plan

Although Germany was strong, she knew her limitations. To avoid a war on two fronts, the German High Command put into motion the Schlieffen Plan, a premeditated strike into France to knock that country out of the war. To avoid France's formidable border defences, the plan also called for German troops to enter France via Belgium, despite the latter country's neutrality. On 3 August 1914, German forces crossed the Belgian border: within a day, Britain had declared war on Germany in support of her allies, France and Belgium, and the Great War had begun.

The Great War

■ Hindenburg's military plans
■ Economic hardship and the armistice

The war had a devastating impact on the countries involved. By the time the **Waffenstillstand** (armistice) was signed on 11 November 1918, millions of men had died in the mud of France, on the cliffs of Gallipoli and through the cold of the eastern front. After the heady enthusiasm of the German nation in 1914, starvation and military defeat had brought the country to its knees. When the USA joined the Allies in 1917 the situation grew even worse. Soldiers and sailors began to mutiny, and for a while it looked as if the events of the Communist Revolution in Russia in 1917 would be repeated in Germany. The military regime under Hindenburg had no choice but to hand over power, but not before the **Kaiser** had been forced to abdicate to fulfil the Allies' terms for the armistice itself. The **zweites Reich** had come to an end.

The Treaty of Versailles

The terms of the Versailles Treaty, imposed on Germany by the Allies in 1919, were so harsh that some of the German High Command immediately urged a new war. **Reichskanzler** Scheidemann knew that this would be total madness, and convinced Parliament to agree to the Treaty's demands. Although this was the only real option available to Germany at the time, the generals were quick to shift the blame for the country's defeat onto the politicians, and thus the **Dolchstoßlegende** (stab-in-the-back legend) was born. Germany settled into this post-war period under a constitution drawn up by the new parliament of the **Weimarer Republik**, but it had little chance to establish itself before the country was again plunged into crisis.

The Weimar Republic: Experiment in democracy

- ■ Kapp putsch
- ■ Rising inflation

There were many people who were not prepared to give democracy a chance. In 1920 the Kapp putsch attempted to depose the government. Although it eventually failed, the fact that the Army initially refused to act to defend the government was a serious development. More and more groups and movements, often formed by disgruntled soldiers who could find no work, rose up in different cities throughout the country. Each was put down, but each time the army became more of a law unto itself (a 'Staat im Staate', or 'state within the state' as one observer commented), especially when the anarchic right-wing **Freikorps** troops were used. Even party politics, supposedly the constitutional means of guaranteeing peace in Germany, became increasingly polarised on the extreme left and right as Communists and Nationalists fought on the streets.

In the midst of all these problems, the German economy was being hit hard because of the harsh reparations forced upon it by the Versailles Treaty. When France marched into the Ruhr in 1923 to ensure payments, the German economy went into a slump. The government had little choice but to devalue the **Mark**, often printing new values onto existing notes. Although this measure solved the short-term problem, inflation now spiralled out of control. The conditions were ripe for a challenge to the authority of the constitutional government, and there were plenty of groups willing to throw down that challenge.

Adolf Hitler and the Nazi Party

Early days

One group, the **Nationalsozialistische Deutsche Arbeiterpartei** (NSDAP or Nazi Party), was an insignificant collection of right-wing Nationalists and anti-Semites. When their leader, Adolf Hitler, declared an alternative government in Munich on 8 November 1923, nobody took too much notice. The putsch was put down easily enough by the Munich police, and Hitler was sentenced to five years' imprisonment for his part in it. He served far less, and during his time in jail wrote *Mein Kampf* (*My Struggle*), where he outlined his vision of a **tausendjähriges** or **drittes Reich** (1000-year or Third Reich). Despite a period of relative economic growth, thanks to the USA-sponsored programmes of loans and economic aid devised by Dawes and Young, Hitler's calls for a return to the strength of Bismarck's Germany proved increasingly popular. Making much of the old **Dolchstoßlegende**, Hitler convinced many Germans that national renewal was possible under his leadership, which would return Germany to her rightful place at the head of Europe. Many rich and influential people began to believe in him, while his Brownshirts continued to fight the Communists on the ground. Parliament was powerless to prevent these developments, and as Germany tottered on the edge of civil war in the autumn of 1932, Hindenburg reluctantly invited Hitler to become the next German chancellor. On 30 January 1933 he took office. Hindenburg's old war colleague, Ludendorff, wrote to the president with a prophetic warning: 'I predict that this terrible man will plunge our country into the abyss.... Future generations will curse you in the grave for your action.' By 23 March Hitler had banned all opposition parties and created a one-party state under the leadership of the **Führer**, Hitler himself. The next part of his vision was the expansion of the German empire.

■ Allied appeasement
■ The Second World War and **Blitzkrieg**

Despite the Versailles Treaty, Hitler prepared for war. In 1936, Germany reoccupied the Rhineland. The same year troops went to the aid of General Franco in the Spanish Civil War. The other European nations desperately tried to appease Hitler, allowing him to annexe the Sudetenland and Austria in 1938, and Bohemia, Slovakia and parts of Lithuania in 1939. While this policy probably bought some time to continue the arms race which had begun in the 1930s, it also convinced Hitler that England in particular had no stomach for war. On 1 September 1939 German troops crossed the Polish border.

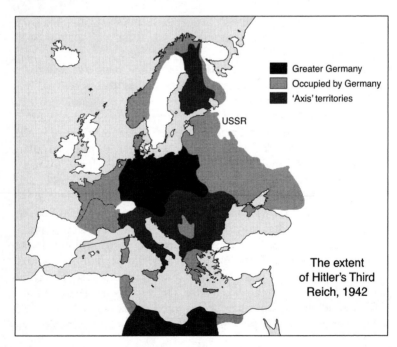

Greater Germany
Occupied by Germany
'Axis' territories

USSR

The extent of Hitler's Third Reich, 1942

Initially, the German **Blitzkrieg** (lightning war) tactics, based around their armoured **Panzer** (tank) divisions, ensured success wherever German troops fought. Poland, Holland, Belgium and France fell in quick succession, and it seemed as if the Soviet Union would crumble within a few months of the invasion in June 1941. But then the USA entered what had become a truly world war, and the tide began to turn against Hitler. For many historians, the destruction of von Paulus' army by Soviet forces at Stalingrad in early 1943 was the decisive moment.

Total defeat and the Holocaust

Once the Allies landed in Normandy on D-Day (6 June 1944) it was really only a matter of time. As the occupied countries were liberated, and Allied troops moved into Germany itself, they came across the **Konzentrationslager** (KZ, concentration camps) such as those at Auschwitz, Belsen and Treblinka. Although their existence had been known for some time, these places revealed the true extent of the Holocaust, the Nazis' attempt to exterminate a whole race of people. The Allied leaders agreed at the Yalta Conference in February 1945 that nothing short of Germany's total capitulation would now be acceptable. In despair, Hitler committed suicide on 30 April, as Soviet troops fought their way into the heart of Berlin; his successor offered the unconditional surrender the Allies wanted on 8 May 1945, and the Third Reich lay in ruins.

Soviet troops hoist their flag atop the *Reichstag* in Berlin.

Two German republics

■ Zones of occupation
■ Cold War and Iron Curtain
■ *Bundesrepublik Deutschland* and *Deutsche Demokratische Republik*

At the Yalta Conference Churchill, Stalin, Roosevelt and de Gaulle had decided that Germany would be split into four zones of control, with each ally controlling a specific area. Britain was given control of the north of Germany, France the Ruhr, Alsace and the west, and America the southern states, including Bavaria. The Soviet Union was then given the whole of the Eastern part of the country, known as the **Sowjetische Besatzungszone** (SBZ) or Soviet Occupation Zone. Berlin, deep inside the SBZ, was itself subdivided. The intention was to allow each of the four powers to strip their zone of industrial materials as part of the reparations Germany would pay for this, second, world war. They would also assist in the 'denazification' of the country. Political parties, banned by the Nazis, were to be allowed to campaign again, a free press was to be established, and the country would be allowed a limited form of self-government. Unfortunately, growing antagonism between the western countries and the Soviet Union meant that these processes developed in very different ways on both sides of the 'Iron Curtain', as Churchill described the line between the western powers and the East. In the West, at least, America poured money into rebuilding the shattered cities, as part of the Marshall Plan to encourage economic growth in western Europe. Having seen the end of one war, Germany was now the ideological battlefield for a new, **kalter Krieg** (Cold War).

Inevitably the two halves of Germany were going in different directions, and the **Bundesrepublik Deutschland** (BRD, Federal Republic, or West Germany) was founded on 23 May 1949. The Soviets responded by founding the **Deutsche Demokratische Republik** (DDR, Democratic Republic, or East Germany) on 7 October 1949. For the West, the BRD was the bulwark against Communism, while the East considered the DDR the flagship of Socialism.

■ The Berlin Wall
■ Willi Brandt and **Ostpolitik**

Throughout the Cold War, relations between the two Germanies were tense. An uprising of protestors throughout East Germany on 17 June 1953 was brutally put down by Soviet tanks, and passions ran high as the West watched the regime clamp down on its dissidents. On 13 August 1961 the people of Berlin woke up to find a wall being built through the middle of their city. For several tense hours American and Russian tanks squared up to each other as East German border guards unrolled miles of barbed wire, poured tons of concrete and piled bricks high upon each other. Eventually a chain of defensive positions stretched across Berlin, and right along the East-West border too. With **die Mauer** (although the term can refer to any wall, all Germans know which one you are talking about when it is spoken with the right tone), the two Germanies were totally divided. Officials in the East declared that the Wall was designed to protect their citizens from the bad influences of the West, and it is certainly true that the Socialist regime was being undermined by West Germany's aggressive and successful economic policies, not to mention the 'brain drain' of educated professionals crossing to the West.

Relations between the BRD and the DDR only began to improve under Willi Brandt after he was elected **Bundeskanzler** (Federal Chancellor) in 1969. His more conciliatory, realistic **Ostpolitik** (literally 'East politics') meant that the two Germanies at least formally recognised each other (for years, schoolchildren in West Germany were taught to refer to the East as 'die sogenannte DDR', the 'so-called GDR'). Technically, the constitution of both Germanies had always allowed for the possibility of reunification, but it was to be another 20 years before that possibility became a reality. In the meantime, life continued in West and East. The West German **Wirtschaftswunder** (economic miracle) of the 1950s had created an economic climate which continued to boom, with very few blips, until West Germany was the economic heart of the **Europäische Wirtschaftsgesellschaft** (EWG, the European Economic Community).

Problems for democracy

Not everything went smoothly for the young democracy, however. The late 1960s saw a powerful and influential student protest movement grow up, resulting in street protests and open revolt in 1968. Still more serious was the government's response to the terrorist **Rote Armee Faktion** (Red Army Faction, or RAF) in the 1960s and 1970s. This ultra-left-wing group, commonly known as the Baader-Meinhoff gang after two of their leaders, began a brutal campaign of bombing department stores and kidnapping prominent industrialists, often with bloody results. In conditions of near-hysteria, the government harshly clamped down on all forms of protest, legitimate or otherwise, and for a while the state of democracy seemed to be in jeopardy. Although the problem eventually disappeared, the suicide in prison of Ulrike Meinhoff in 1972 seemed too convenient to many observers. One unfortunate side-effect of this period was that the state ignored the rise of right-wing neo-Nazi groups, which have persisted in Germany throughout the 1980s and 1990s.

Reunification

The *Wende* and post-reunification troubles

The pictures of East and West Berliners clambering over the Wall in November 1989 brought rejoicing all around the world, not just

East and West meet atop the Berlin Wall.

in Germany. In the months leading up to that night, the East German regime had been steadily losing its grip on the state, and Gorbachev's Soviet Union had already indicated that it would do nothing to prop up its troubled ally. After fears of terrible reprisals (images of tanks crushing protestors on China's Tianamen Square were still fresh in the memory), suddenly the path was clear, quite literally, for contact between East and West Berlin. On 3 October 1990 the people of two Germanies, divided for a generation, celebrated the **Wiedervereinigung** (reunification) of their country.

But it was not all plain sailing, and the reunified Germany has had many problems coping with the **Wende**, as this period has come to be known (the word literally means 'turnaround'). The DDR was in serious financial difficulties at the end, and the **alte Bundesländer** (the West German states) have had to pay far more than most expected to keep the new **Länder** afloat. Rising unemployment and pressure from extreme right-wing elements meant that discontent grew. Although the physical Wall was gone, people now spoke of a new **Mauer im Kopf** (Wall in the head).

As a general election loomed in 1998 it became clear that the German people were ready for change. On 27 September Helmut Kohl, the longest serving German chancellor since Bismarck, lost to a more youthful Gerhard Schröder. Schröder was elected on promises of an end to rising unemployment and a solution to the problems of the East. Whether he can deliver on his promises remains to be seen.

The German nation was a long time in establishing itself, and on more than one occasion in its complex history seemed to be moving apart rather than towards unity. Although the post-**Wende** period of German history is almost certainly not over, it seems likely that whatever comes next, Germany in its current form will continue playing a central role in European matters for a very long time.

GLOSSARY

die Landeskarte (-n) *map*
die Ostsee *the Baltic Sea*
die Nordsee *the North Sea*
das Bundesland (-länder) *federal state*
der Wald (ˉr) *woods, forest*
der Fluss (ˉe) *river*
der Berg (-e) *mountain*
das Gebirge *mountains*
im Norden/Osten/Süden/Westen
 in the north/east/south/west
die Grenze (-n) *border*

der Krieg (-e) *war*
der Bürger (-) *citizen*
das Reich *empire*
der Frieden *peace*
die Politik *politics*
das Land (ˉer) *country*
das Volk (Völker) *inhabitants,*
 population, the people
die Geschichte *history*
der Nationalismus *nationalism*
die (Wieder-) Vereinigung
 (re-) unification

Taking it further

Any guide to Germany is likely to give you further information on
Germany's landscape and history, but you might like to try the
Lonely Planet Guide to Germany, or the *APA Insight Guide:
Germany*. If history is your particular interest, try Martin Kitchen's
Cambridge Illustrated History of Germany (1996) or *A Concise
History of Germany* (1990, 1992) by Mary Fulbrook.

If you have internet access, try www.web.de, which is a useful mix
of entertainment, weather reports and other information, with a
good search engine ... but it is entirely in German. Similarly, the
Deutsches Historisches Museum in Berlin has an excellent web
site, with English and German pages, plus a very interesting
'virtual tour' through German history (currently in German). The
museum is closed until 2002 for extensive work, but let the web
site give you a taste of what's to come. The address is
www.dhm.de.

2 THE GERMAN LANGUAGE

You may have noticed that different languages have vastly different words for 'German' and 'Germany': the French say 'Allemagne/ allemand', the Russian for 'German' is 'nemetz/nemetski', and the Italian 'tedesco'. This may have something to do with the various tribes which contributed to the German race. The Germans, on the other hand, say '**Deutschland/deutsch**', which actually originates in the language spoken by all the tribes: *teutsch*.

Aspects of modern German

A world language?

It is probably fair to say that German is *not* a world language in the same sense as English or Spanish. There are, nevertheless, areas of speech where German has had a great effect: many English speakers would recognise words like **Doppelgänger** (human double), **Weltanschauung** (attitude to the world) or **Blitzkrieg** (lightning war), which have been borrowed by English. For much of the 18th and 19th centuries, German was probably the main language of science and philosophy, simply because all the leading work in those fields was being produced by German speakers.

Of course, German is not spoken by just the inhabitants of Germany, either – we must not forget the German-speaking states of Austria and Lichtenstein, or that roughly a third of the population of Switzerland speak a dialect of German as their mother-tongue. Less well known is the fact that the majority of the population of northern Italy is German-speaking, and that there are sizeable minority German communities in the Czech Republic,

Poland and several states belonging to the former Soviet Union. All in all it is estimated that some 100 million people speak German as a native tongue. Moreover, Yiddish is closely related to German, as are the low German languages of Dutch and Flemish, and (to a lesser extent) the Scandinavian tongues.

The Goethe-Institut

The responsibility for promoting the language to the rest of the world lies with a body known as the Goethe-Institut. With 150 branches right across the globe, the Goethe-Institut promotes links with Germany, organises cultural and educational exchanges, and supports teachers of German in the host country.

Dialects and minority languages in Germany

Technically, the sort of German a foreigner learns at nightschool or through a cassette course is known as **Hochdeutsch**, or High German. We will go into exactly what that means shortly, but essentially this is the equivalent of 'BBC English', namely a standard form of the language taught in German schools and spoken by all German people, albeit with regional accents. For many, however, this is less important than their own particular **Dialekt**. These dialects have largely flourished in Germany, probably because of the fragmented nature of the country's history. Although some people bemoan the slow demise of many dialects, many more survive and flourish: **Plattdeutsch** in the north and on the Dutch border, **Sächsisch** in Saxony, **Kölsch** around Cologne, **Schwäbisch** in the south-west, not forgetting **Bayrisch** in Bavaria. For the most part these dialects are languages in their own right, sufficiently removed from **Hochdeutsch** that a family speaking at the dinner table in, say, **Platt** will not be understood at all by someone from outside the region.

Having said that, there is only one true minority language in Germany. In the region of Bautzen, to the east of Dresden, the language of **Sorbisch** is still spoken by a small community of about 100,000. Nobody is entirely sure where Sorbian came from, although it is a Slav language related to Czech and Slovak. The Sorb community was swallowed up by the expanding Germanic tribes in the 7th century, and has been clinging to its unique culture and customs ever since. Although the German authorities did little to help the language until recent years, there are now schools teaching Sorbian, and public and road signs in the area are increasingly bilingual.

The German language

What of the German language itself? Usually when talking about German, people will mention two clichés: one is that the language is very harsh to the ear, and the other is that German is extremely difficult to learn.

Certainly it is fair to say that German can be quite a challenging language for the non-native – indeed, German children find it pretty tough when they learn it at school. But there are some aspects of German which make it a very straightforward language to learn. Spellings and pronounciation are generally very easy to learn, for instance, and (as you might expect from the Germans?) the grammar is very logical on the whole. In other words, don't let people put you off when they knock German! Let's look at some of the most interesting points about the language.

Gender

All German nouns have one of three genders, masculine, feminine or neuter. This gender is reflected in the articles (English 'the' and 'a') which change according to which gender a noun has. So masculine nouns use **der**, feminine nouns **die**, and neuter nouns **das**. While some words have a pretty logical gender, because a person is clearly male (e.g. **der Mann**, man) or female (**die Ärztin**, lady doctor) others are totally illogical, or have a gender which reflects a linguistic consideration (for instance, **das Mädchen**, girl, is neuter). There is very little consistency even when a group of words belong to a related category, so **Löffel**, spoon, **Gabel**, fork, and **Messer**, knife are actually masculine (**der**), feminine (**die**) and neuter (**das**) respectively!

Case

As if this weren't confusing enough, there are four cases in German: nominative, accusative, genitive and dative. Each time a noun or adjective is used in one of these cases, the form of the article has to change, as does any adjectival ending associated with the noun. This is probably the most confusing apect of the language for the non-native, but it does pay to persevere, because eventually you 'tune in' to the language and get an ear for what sounds right.

Word order

One final point worth mentioning here is that the word order of a sentence can be quite interesting, too. As well as one rule which says that a verb form should always be the second idea in a sentence **Eines Tages | ging <-|-> Janet | zu den Läden** ('one day

| *went* <-|-> Janet | to the shops'), it is also vital that any extra verbs are placed at the very end of the sentence **ich | bin | nach Amerika | gefahren** ('I | *have* | to America | *travelled*').

As for the charge that German is a very harsh language, well, that really depends on your ear! Certainly German is full of sounds which are not very common in English. Many words contain, or end in, unusual combinations of letters, such as **-ich** and **-ig**, **-ung** and **-keit**, and some look unpronounceable at first (the combinations **-pf-** or **-tz-** being good examples). But it is all a matter of **Übung macht den Meister** (practice makes perfect, or literally, practice makes the master), so if you are thinking of learning German, or have recently started, don't be put off! One of the aims of this book is to introduce you to the many and varied aspects of Germany's culture which can be unlocked for you if you learn to speak to the natives.

The origins of the German language

Indo-European: the father of German

Like most European languages, the roots of German are said to be found in 'Indo-European'. But it is only in the 500 years or so leading up to the birth of Christ that German, or perhaps 'Germanic' begins to evolve in its own right. A series of changes, known as the first Germanic shift, see words like the Latin *pater* (father) become the Gothic *vadar*, while the Greek word *thura* (door) evolves into the Gothic *daur*.

German and other Germanic languages

ca. 7th–10th centuries AD: Old High German

Later, during the historically important **Völkerwanderung** (people's migration), the Germanic tribes scattered to different parts of Europe. In Germany proper there was a second sound shift, allowing English (which was cut off by the Channel) to develop as a related, but separate, language. At the same time, other Germanic languages resisted the changes in the areas which came to be Dutch and Danish speaking, for instance.

Althochdeutsch, or Old High German, as the new language came to be called, was now a language in its own right, and developed some of the sound and letter combinations we recognise today. So while the Gothic word *punt* led to the English word 'pound', in German it changed to *Pfund*; similarly the Gothic *wappe* developed into the English 'weapon', but shifted to the German *Waffe* (with the initial 'w' eventually becoming a 'v' sound).

Medieval German and the development of a 'national' language

12th–14th centuries AD: Middle High German

In the early medieval period there was still no one single German language. Gradually, however, increased contact between the different regions in Germany led to a more standardised **Mittelhochdeutsch**, or Middle High German (MHG). This was the time when the German double-dot accent called **Umlaut** ('change in sound'), came about.

14th–17th centuries AD: Early New High German

Despite this standardisation there was still a linguistic battle going on between the different regions. Three major dialects were involved: 'Low' German was spoken in the north, on the Baltic coast, in the Hanseatic towns and in the German Low Countries; 'Central' German was spoken in the powerful regions of Saxony and Leipzig; southern 'Upper' German was to be heard in Bavaria and the Habsburg (later Austrian) states. All other areas gradually adopted one of these three, although some regions resisted change for years – indeed, some dialects of German have still not adopted all the changes, notably Swiss.

■ Martin Luther's Bible
■ The influence of printing

It was Martin Luther's German New Testament in 1522, and Bible in 1534, which ensured that his Saxon version of German quickly spread throughout the country. This would not have been possible had it not been for the development of the moveable printing press by Johannes Gutenberg in 1445. Between 1500 and 1550 the number of households which owned a Bible rocketed from just over 1 per cent to over 30 per cent. As a growing number of middle-class merchants and citizens looked to buy and read books without the advantage of a formal, Latin-based education, the success of German as a literary language, and of Luther's central German dialect as a convenient standard, was guaranteed. With the rise of the universities the study of the German tongue was formalised and academics began to write the first grammar texts. In 1687 Christian Thomasius became one of the first academics to deliver lectures in German, at Leipzig University. Although he was promptly expelled from the university for this outrage, by 1710 the majority of lectures in Germany's universities were delivered in the native tongue.

Modern German

■ 18th century AD – present: High German
■ The German language and national identity

As the German peoples became more aware of their shared cultural heritage in the late 1700s and 1800s, so the notion of the German language being a common bond grew. In *Reden an die deutsche Nation* (*Addresses to the German Nation*, 1808/09) Johann Fichte reacted to Germany's humiliating occupation by Napoleon with an impassioned appeal to the German people to view their language as part of their unique nature.

The Brothers Grimm and Konrad Duden

In the aftermath of this awakening interest in national identity, the Grimm brothers, renowned for recording many of the folk tales which had hitherto existed only in the oral tradition, engaged themselves with the fundamentals of the German language. Jakob Grimm wrote a systematic study of German, called *'das Grimmsche Gesetz'* (the Grimm laws) which attempted to explain the language in a series of scientific explanations. A little later, in 1872, Konrad Duden published *Die deutsche Rechtschreibung* (*Correct Written German*) which aimed to create a convention for all aspects of the language. The text proved so popular that it is still published today, with regular updates.

Language reform

As the 19th century came to an end and the 20th began, so it became more and more desirable to ensure that every aspect of the language should be governed by rules and regulations, and to iron out any remaining discrepancies of usage or convention. A series of conferences, beginning in 1876, brought about the regulation of spellings, debates on **Großschreibung** (the use of capitals at the beginning of all nouns, which had developed in the 17th and 18th centuries), the gender of nouns, and all conceivable issues relating to the German language. One major concern was the rapid influx of English loan words, particularly after the end of the Second World War. Some decisions were relatively simple, because they merely rubber-stamped accepted practice. Others, however, were far more arbitrary and controversial, and the changes they introduced were then resisted by one or more of the regions. At the Wiesbaden conference in 1950, therefore, representatives of Germany, Austria and Switzerland agreed on the principal of unanimity for any further changes.

Two Germanies and foreign loan words

The division of Germany after the Second World War saw some interesting developments in the language. These were largely restricted to the realms of vocabulary usage or, crucially, to opposing definitions of the same word. While West Germans readily took to words like **Teenager**, **Jeans** or **Bobbysoxers**, dictionaries in the East refused to list them, preferring instead **Kollektiv** (collective farm), **Datscha** (country house, usually for senior party members) or **Held der Arbeit** (literally, Hero of Work). Whereas a West German dictionary would define the word **Demokratie** as the will of the people, or the opposite of **Diktatur**, an East German one would stress the necessity of **Sozialismus** to achieve true democracy. Likewise, **Ideologie**, while being considered dangerous in the West, was accepted in the East as part and parcel of political life. For a while the antagonism even extended to a refusal by Duden, in the West, to include DDR words such as **Volksarmee** (People's Army) or **Brigade** (the collective term for a group of factory workers). By the time the Wall fell in 1989 the two German languages had not really had enough time to change in any meaningful way.

1998: die Rechtschreibreform

In the period following the **Wende** it was decided to convene a committee of academics, writers, politicians and other public figures from all the German-speaking countries to see whether the time was ripe for **Rechtschreibreform** (orthographic reform, or reform of written German). Theoretically, nothing was sacrosanct: from **Großschreibung** (capitalisation) to the **Esszet/scharfes S** (the double s – ß – symbol), from spellings of loan words to the use of commas.

In July 1996 the committee finally published its recommendations in Vienna. A proposal to drop the **Esszet** altogether (to bring the other countries in line with Switzerland, which already uses **-ss-** all the time), was dropped in the end, but all the other recommendations were, theoretically, designed to make the language simpler and more logical. The **Esszet** rules were, at least, simplified, as were many of the complicated comma rules (the bane of German children and foreign learners of German alike). Furthermore, a whole range of spellings were recommended for simplification and/or consistency (see box for examples). The committee proposed a date of 1 August 1998 for the introduction of the new rules, with a five-year period of grace to allow a relatively painless transition for those who had learned the old rules.

Die deutsche Rechtschreibreform, 1996: A summary

Some examples of the changes introduced on 1 August 1998:

■ **Spelling of foreign loan words**

e.g. Delphin *dolphin*   becomes   Delfin
Saxophon *saxophone*   →   Saxofon

■ **Compounds**

e.g. Schifffahrt *ship travel* →   Schiff-Fahrt
schwerverständlich   →   schwer verständlich
barely comprehensible

■ *ss* **and** *ß*

e.g. Fluß *river*   →   Fluss
er/sie ißt *he/she eats* →   isst
daß *that*   →   dass

These are examples only, and do not show all the changes, nor the remaining exceptions. For further guidance see e.g. *Die deutsche Rechtschreibung* (Duden Verlag, 21st Edition, 1996), from which all the examples given above are taken.

The **Reform** was met with storms of protest. Ironically, many felt that the changes had not gone far enough, merely tinkering with the language rather than genuinely simplifying it. Many of the **Länder** announced that they would oppose the changes, and private cases were brought against the reform in the **Bundesverfassungsgericht** (Federal Constitutional Court, the highest legal body in the land – see Chapter 8 for more details). Even now popular resistance to the reforms is strong. Many ordinary German adults, in particular, are very upset at the thought of having to unlearn the various rules and spellings which they struggled over as children, but the fact that the new forms are now taught by default in the majority of German-speaking schools means that they are likely to filter into society at large in due course: it is worth bearing in mind, however, that the metric system of measurements has been taught in schools in Great Britain since the early 1970s and is still far from replacing the older imperial system of weights and measures. It is very hard to force a country to change! Also, it is true to say that the German language has, historically speaking, always resisted attempts to impose changes artificially. The first few decades of the 21st century are likely to be very interesting for the impartial observer of the German language!

GLOSSARY

die deutsche Sprache *the German language*
Deutsch *German*
Deutsch lernen *to learn German*

Hochdeutsch *High German*
sprechen *to speak*
der Dialekt (-e) *dialect*

Taking it further

If you want to learn German you might like to contact your local nightschool, or adult learning centre. There are also many hundreds of audio-visual and CD-Rom courses available to help you learn the language on your own. If you're not sure where to start, try the Goethe-Institut, where someone will be happy to give you advice on how to go about it. The address of the London branch is given here, but you should find one in virtually every capital in the world, and many other major cities.

Goethe Institut UK
50 Princes Gate
Exhibition Road
London SW7 2PH
Tel: (0171) 596 4000
Web site: http://www.goethe.de/london

3 | LITERATURE AND PHILOSOPHY

It would perhaps be true to say that not many people think of Germany as a literary centre of any great importance. There may be any number of reasons for this, not least of which is the great standing of English and French literature throughout the world. Indeed, the Germans themselves have often considered their home-grown literary efforts to be inferior to those of their close neighbours, and have taken great British and French authors and thinkers as their role-models. Nevertheless there have, in every age, been some outstanding men and women writing in German, and at times works produced in Germany have been at the forefront of world literature.

Over and above this discussion, it should be stressed that an understanding of a nation's literary and philosophical efforts can grant you unique insights into the culture in question. This is partly because we see intimate pictures of the way the people live their lives in that country, but also because we can also learn something of the way they would like to be, or wish they had been in the past. Even if you are a relative beginner in learning the German language, there are so many good translations of important literary works from Germany that it should be an easy matter to find out a little more about what makes a German tick, through his or her literary heritage.

8th–10th century AD: The origins of German literature

The earliest texts

Not surprisingly, it is a little difficult to say with any real confidence exactly when the first works of German literature appeared. As early as the 4th century the Visigoth Bishop Wulfila had produced a translation of the Greek Bible in his native Gothic, and there is evidence to suggest that there was a rich tradition of oral storytelling in German, some of which might have been committed to paper.

Much of the work produced at this early period was still translations of Latin religious works, but the survival of the Old High German epic poem *Das Hildebrandslied* (*Song of Hildebrand*, written sometime after 750) is an early example of a German-language narrative. The manuscript in our possession was written in the monastery at Fulda around 840. It tells of a fight to the death between the great warrior Hildebrand and his son Hadubrand, and portrays a world where a rigid code of honour and duty is the cement which keeps their society from slipping into chaos.

Mittelhochdeutsch

The next work of major significance is the *Rolandslied* (*Song of Roland*), written after the French version by Chrétien de Troyes. It is an exhortation to live a God-fearing life in the same way that the hero, none other than King Charlemagne himself, once did when he brought Christianity to the heathens. We know that the tale was written down in the middle decades of the 12th century, by a priest called Konrad, because he mentions himself at one point in the story: '*Ich haize der phaffe Chunrat*' ('My name is priest Konrad'). Significantly, too, the use of the term '*riter*' (here refering to the soldiers in the story) was soon to be associated exclusively with the noble knight, around whom German medieval literature was centred for the next several hundred years.

12th–14th century: Early medieval literature

Middle High German, *Minnesang* and the age of chivalry

The ideals of chivalry, nobility, loyalty and honour were elevated to the central tenets of German culture in the Middle Ages. The first great German literary movement, known as **Minnesang** (love poetry) was born out of the crusades and the chivalric life. Lesser knights made a living between campaigns by travelling about the country as troubadours, living off the patronage of more powerful noblemen and singing their praises in court. Their poetry contains motifs of honour and service, mixed with references to noble ladies and the (usually unrequited) love of the lesser knights for these unattainable beauties. Of all the **Minnesänger**, Walther von der Vogelweide (ca. 1170 – ca. 1230) is considered the best, and he was

certainly one of the most prolific, and most imitated. This new art form achieved a level of complexity hitherto unknown in German, with its subtle metaphors of love and honour as common as more straightforward descriptions of a particular woman's great beauty. A good example is this extract, by an Austrian knight known as '*Der von Kürenberg*' (The One from Kürenberg'), where the poem can be taken at face value, or can be read as a reference to a woman who has been wooed and lost:

Ich zôch mir einen valken mêre danne ein jâr.
dô ich in gezamete,   als ich in wolte hân,
und ich im sîn gevidere   mit golde wol bewant,
er huop sich ûf vil hôhe   und fluoc in ándèriu lant.

(I reared a falcon for more than a year.
And when I had tamed him just as I wanted him,
and wanted to wind gold into his feathers,
he took off up into the sky and flew to other lands.)

Epic fiction

Another group of nobles were producing epic tales of the common legends current at that time in western Europe. Hartmann von Aue (ca.1165–ca.1215), wrote **Der arme Heinrich** (*Poor Henry*) in about1195, based on Arthurian legends. The lesson of the tale was that human values are flimsy in the face of God's eternal truth. The noble '*herre Heinrich*' learns that '*êre unde guot*' (honour and goodness) are gifts from God, which ought not be taken for granted. Gottfried von Strassburg (died ca. 1210) earned great accolades with **Tristan**, a version of the love story of Tristan and Isolde. He thrills his audience with the racy material, suggesting '*Ir leben ir tot sint unser brot*' ('Their life, their death, are bread to us'). Finally Wolfram von Eschenbach (ca.1170-ca.1220) produced one of the great works of his era, in the epic **Parzifal** (ca. 1200). Consisting of around 25,000 lines of highly accomplished poetry, **Parzifal** is another Grail story, which sings the praises of the courtly virtues so central to the society of this age.

The *Nibelungenlied*

The **Nibelungenlied** (*Song of the Nibelungs*), written around 1200, is considered probably the finest piece of early German literature. Like the Old English epic *Beowulf*, it is a vitally important glimpse into a much older oral tradition of storytelling and as such it never fails to capture the imagination of Germans, even today. (Of course, it also forms the framework for Wagner's opera cycle, written more than 700 years later.) The **Nibelungenlied** sprawls across some 39 separate *Aventiure* (adventures, the origin of the modern German word **Abenteuer**) and contains elements of love, jealousy, intrigue, fights and revenge. The opening lines tell of the breadth of the tale:

Uns ist in alten maeren
wunders vil geseit
von helden lobebaeren,
von grôzer arebeit,
von fröuden, hôchgeziten,
von weinen und von klagen,
von küener recken striten
muget ir nu wunderhoeren sagen.

(To us is told in tales of old
Of many wondrous things:
Of heroes and their valour,
Of great deeds,
Of joys and of celebrations,
Of tears and of laments,
Of bold knights' clashes,
May you now hear of these wonders.)

Classics of German literature: The *Nibelungenlied*

This epic adventure, which also reveals so much about the medieval German psyche, was the inspiration for Wagner's famous opera cycle in the 20th century (see Chapter 5).

The tale is laid out in a series of adventures: the first 18 relate the background against which all the action takes place, and describe the relationship between the different tribes and characters around which the story is woven. They then describe how Siegfried woos the beautiful Kriemhilde and eventually wins her hand in marriage. He is then betrayed and murdered by Hagen. In the nineteenth adventure, the treasure of the Nibelungs is cast into the Rhine to prevent it falling into the wrong hands, and in the final section (adventures 20 to 29) we see Kriemhilde's revenge for the murder of her husband, which culminates in the bloody end of the Burgundians, and of Kriemhilde herself.

The Reformation and beyond

For the next 400 years there were few developments of note, although the Reformation did see the first signs of Humanism (discussion of the nature of God, and of man's relationship with God). One important work appeared in 1669, when Hans Jakob von Grimmelshausen (1622–1676) published *Der abentheuerliche Simplicissimus Teutsch* (*The Adventurous Simplicissimus Teutsch*). After the destruction of the Thirty Years' War (which plays an important role in the novel itself), *Simplicissimus* was a runaway hit in its own day, needing reprints soon after its first appearance. It is important because it is a picaresque tale, meaning that the reader is invited to associate with the hero, and to follow him through a series of adventures and experiences which lead him to a certain conclusion. Here, we watch Simplicius, who is separated from his parents at the beginning of the war, develop into an older and wiser adult. He travels around the world, serves different masters, and fights in various battles around Europe until the war is over and he can settle down to a quieter life. Critics believe that the novel contains many autobiographical elements, but it is nevertheless quite clearly a work of entertainment which set a standard German fiction had not seen before, and struggled to achieve in subsequent years.

18th century: Germany, land of *Dichter und Denker*

■ The Age of Enlightenment
■ Rejection of the classics

After several hundred years which produced little work of any note, the 18th century saw a boom of genuine creativity and innovation. It was during this time that Germany came to be known as the nation of **Dichter und Denker** (translated as 'poets and thinkers', although **Dichter** is a broader term than the English, which describes people who write poetry alone). The **Aufklärung** (Enlightenment) in Germany began this process. Philosophers such as Gottfried Leibniz (1646–1716) and Immanuel Kant (1724–1804) began openly to question the relevance of religion and look instead to the individual's experiences. They, in turn, inspired a whole generation of writers to turn their backs on the Greek and Latin classics and produce a new, vibrant, German literature.

German authors such as Johann Gottsched (1700–1766) and Gotthold Ephraim Lessing (1729–81) enthusiastically created new kinds of plays and novels, full of German heroes and heroines who busily go about their intensely subjective lives. Sophie von la Roche (1731–1807) married the English middle-class novel with the particularly German notion of man in his natural environment. In *Geschichte des Fräuleins von Sternheim* (*History of Miss von Sternheim*, 1771), a **Briefroman** (novel in letter form) which was a great commercial success at the time, von la Roche traced the fortunes of a heroine who suffers great misfortune early in her life but eventually finds happiness. Along the way she comes to acknowledge the vital role played by nature in developing man (and woman): '**Die Natur selbst habe, in der Leidenschaft der Liebe, den Mann heftig, die Frau zärtlich gemacht**' ('Nature has, in the passions of love, made man forceful, and woman tender').

■ **Sturm und Drang**
■ **Weimarer Klassik**

One group went even further in linking man with his environment and portraying him at the mercy of his own, subjective emotions. The **Sturm und Drang** (Storm and Yearning) movement was gathered together in Johann Herder's anthology *Von deutscher Art und Kunst* (*Of German Style and Art*, 1773), including some work by the young Johann Wolfgang von Goethe.

Goethe published his first work, *Die Leiden des jungen Werthers* (*The Suffering of Young Werther*) in 1774. It is another **Briefroman**, and initially appears to offer another pleasant portrait of man at one with his natural surroundings. At one point he writes: '**Ich bin allein und freue mich meines Lebens in dieser Gegend, die für solche Seelen geschaffen ist wie die meine**' ('I am quite alone and rejoice in my life in this region, which has been created for such souls as mine'). However, it transpires that Werther's soul is equally at home with melancholy. The story follows his decline into despair, fuelled by an unrequited love, which eventually leads to his suicide. The book became an instant bestseller, and it became something of a fad to affect Werther's style of dress in a blue frock coat and yellow waistcoat.

Johann Wolfgang von Goethe, for many Germany's greatest man of letters.

Goethe was based in Weimar at this time, which quickly became an important centre of literary pre-eminence in Germany, and Europe at large. Central to this success were Goethe and another enterprising author, Friedrich Schiller. Schiller's play *Die Räuber* (*The Robbers*, 1782) became an international hit in its own right. What these two men had in common was an unshakeable belief in the ability of the German language to compete with other literary languages on equal terms. Goethe proved this most conclusively with his classic drama of *Faust*.

Classics of German literature 2: Goethe's *Faust*

The play that is referred to as *Faust* is in reality more than a single play, and is based on a story already more than 200 years old. (Christopher Marlowe had used the same material for his English-language *Dr Faustus* in the late 1500s.) Goethe himself created a number of variations on the theme, beginning with the version known as *Urfaust* which he wrote between 1772–1775. The final version, *Faust II*, appeared in 1825 and shows the fascination it exerted over Goethe throughout his career. Whichever version you read, certain elements remain fairly constant: Faust is a learned man who is unfulfilled by his quest for earthly knowledge. He consequently enters into a pact with Mephistopheles, who is the Devil personified. Although the episodes related in each version of *Faust* can differ, they all describe the slow slide towards tragedy as Mephistopheles demands his price for the pact. One crucial theme is the ill-fated love affair between Faust and Gretchen, a young girl who dies a tragic death after being used and abused by her lover.

Faust reached new fame after the Second World War, when many people interpreted the play as representative of Germany's willingness to enter into a pact with Hitler. Whether such a reading can be justified or not, the tragedy of the tale has ensured the novel's fame ever since.

19th century: From French Revolution to German unification

The age of revolution

From the end of the 18th century, revolution swept across Europe. The French occupation of Germany led many to debate the nature of war and of the national identity of the still-divided German states. In *Prinz Friedrich von Homburg* (1821), Heinrich von Kleist (1777–1811) attempted to define the nature of the heroic leader and depicted the early days of the Prussian state. Christian Grabbe (1801–1836) approached the same period from a radically different direction. The drama *Napoleon oder die Hundert Tage* (*Napoleon or the Hundred Days*, 1829) followed the fortunes of the notorious leader from the early days of the French Revolution until his final defeat at the hands of Wellington at Waterloo. Significant here, too, is the portrayal of the German soldiers in Wellington's army, united in the common cause: '**Ja, das ganze Heer war wie elektrisch – Berliner und Schlesier, Pommer und Märker, alle eine freudige, aber übergewaltige Glut, sowie es hieß "Auf den Feind!"**' ('Yes, the whole army was as if electrified – Berliners and Schlesians, Pommeranians and Mark Brandenburgians, all one mighty glowing fire as soon as the word came "To the enemy!"').

Germany was not spared Europe's revolutionary spirit, however: Georg Büchner (1813–1837) was politically active in the **Gesellschaft der Menschenrechte** (Society of Human Rights). He launched vicious attacks on society's injustices in *Dantons Tod* (1835) and *Woyzeck* (1836). *Woyzeck*, in particular, became an immensely important work to later dramatists, with the hero being a member of the growing working class, or proletariat, who suffers at the hands of an injust society. Woyzeck is told: '**Du bist ein guter Mensch ... aber du denkst zuviel, das zehrt**' ('You are a good man, but you think too much, it wears you out'). He recognises the truth of his impoverished situation: '**Wir arme Leut. [...] Ich glaub', wenn wir in Himmel kämen, so müßten wir donnern helfen**' ('Us poor people. I reckon even if we got into heaven we would have to help make the thunder').

At the same time, Karl Marx (1818–1883) and Friedrich Engels (1820–1895) were producing a document entitled *Manifest der kommunistischen Partei* (1848). Although it was largely ignored at the time of its publication it did, of course, go on to shape the world we live in. It argued that the proletariat has the power for the very first time to take control of the state in order to ensure a fairer distribution of wealth. It is interesting to note that Marx and Engels never advanced the notion of the 'party', in the sense that we think of Communist governments in our century, while their use of 'state' simply referred to the committee which would carry out the wishes of these newly empowered masses ... and yet this is the manifesto which resulted in the Cold War and the division of Germany into East and West!

Idylls and realities: *Romantik* and *Realismus*

At the end of the 19th century a literary form grew up which has always been considered particularly German. The **Novelle** was a short story which was meant to portray society in a realistic, but critical, light. This **bürgerlicher Realismus** (bourgeois realism) did not feature in all **Novellen**, but it was an important element in a period called Romantic. The north German Theodor Storm (1817–1888) explored most deeply the psychological unrest of his protagonists in, for instance, *Immensee* (*Lake Immensee*, 1850) or *Der Schimmelreiter* (*The White Horse Rider*, 1888). *Der Schimmelreiter,* for many the most celebrated of Germany's **Novellen**, depicts the tension between the old beliefs of a north German community and the technologically advanced Hauke Haien, who is responsible for the dykes and coastal defences in the area. Although Hauke sees his designs for an improved dyke system through to completion, the resentment of the locals and his own contempt for their conservatism end in tragedy: Hauke's family is killed when the sea breaks through the defences, and Hauke himself plunges into the water on his white horse. In later years he is spotted as a ghostly apparition riding across the coastal sands.

The *Gründerzeit*

Towards the end of the 19th century, photography was changing the way people looked at the world. Authors, too, became more objective in their portrayal of society. Theodor Fontane (1819–1898) described the injustices of a rigid society in *Effi Briest* (1894), where the heroine is trapped in a loveless marriage and commits adultery to escape. When her husband discovers the affair he has no choice but to challenge her lover to a duel, in order to save face: the lover is killed. The shifting sands of the area in which she lives not only represent the turmoil of her emotions, caught as she is in a society which condemns her out of hand for her crime, but also lead to her death.

The will to power: Nietzsche

As the century came to an end, Friedrich Nietzsche (1844–1900) put forward the belief that the individual could develop to become master of his own destiny, a super-being more advanced than humans in his own time. The oft-quoted (and much abused) *Jenseits von Gut und Böse* (*Beyond Good and Evil*, 1886) proposed that man, as a flawed being, would have to develop, or he would cease to exist. '**Moral ist heute in Europa Herdentier-Moral**' ('Morals in today's Europe are the morals of the herd'). Without an incentive to change, Nietzsche believed, mankind was doomed; he called for '**eine neue Art von Philosophen und Befehlshabern**' (a new kind of philosophers and commanders) who would rise up from the herd and begin the process of renewal. It was the **Wille zur Macht** (Will to Power) which would attract these new humans to act, and which was seized on by the Nazis in the 1930s, despite the fact that Nietzsche also stressed the moral responsibility of his theories.

From Expressionism to the Weimar Republic

Turn of the century trends: modern German literature

The **Jahrhundertwende** (turn of the century) saw German literature break new ground, inspired by the sexual theories of the Austrian Sigmund Freud. The play *Frühlingserwachen* (*Spring Awakening*, 1891) by Frank Wedekind (1864-1918) contained explicit references to, and scenes of, aberrant sexuality, which were calculated to highlight the repressive nature of sexuality in Germany at the time. Similarly, Wedekind's later play *Die Büchse der Pandora* (*Pandora's Box*, 1904) depicted an innocent girl who is forced into prostitution by society's sexual hypocrisy, and is finally killed by a serial murderer.

One of the most significant authors of the new century was Thomas Mann (1875–1955). His most famous work was the huge novel *Buddenbrooks* (1901), which described the fate of one merchant family in Lübeck over the course of several generations. It was a frank portrayal of the lives of the characters and remains a popular novel even today.

Classics of German literature 3: *Buddenbrooks*, by Thomas Mann

The subtitle of Thomas Mann's 1901 novel reveals much about the story it relates: *Verfall einer Familie* (*Decline of a Family*). Four generations of a merchant family from Lübeck are followed, against the backdrop of the second half of the 19th century.

The first character, Johann Buddenbrook, represents the solid tradition of **Bürgertum** (bourgeois values), which allow him to build his empire. His four grandchildren, however, Thomas, Christian, Tony (a girl) and Clara, all represent aspects of private and social decline. Although Thomas, as the eldest, seems to continue the traditions of the previous generations, spiced with the teachings of Schopenhauer, it transpires that much of his success is artificial. He dies as a result of complications during a dental procedure, leaving a son. Hanno Buddenbrook, then, presides over the demise of the family, representing the end of the patrician families which made the north German **Hansestädte** so prosperous.

Expressionism

Of all the 20th century literary movements in Germany, Expressionism was probably the most productive of all, throwing up two of Germany's most famous authors, Franz Kafka (1883–1924) and Bertolt Brecht (1898–1956). Kafka wrote some of the most profound and most disturbing stories ever written in any language – so much so that the word 'kafkaesque' has come to mean 'unfathomable', or 'deeply bizarre'. In *Der Prozeß* (*The Trial*, 1914), Josef K. stands accused of a crime, but is unable to determine either the crime he is supposed to have committed or the identity or authority of the court that tries him. Even worse is the fate of Gregor Samsa in *Die Verwandlung* (*Metamorphosis*, 1916): **'Als Gregor Samsa eines Morgens aus unruhigen Träumen erwachte, fand er sich in seinem Bett zu einem ungeheueren Ungeziefer verwandelt'** ('When Gregor Samsa woke up one morning from disturbing dreams, he found himself in his bed, transformed into a monstrous creature'). Unable to feed himself, but equally unable to make his family aware of his plight, Gregor dies a squalid death in his room, all alone.

Bert Brecht first came to public attention with his plays *Baal* (1919) and *Trommeln in der Nacht* (*Drums in the Night*, 1919) which set the tone for his cynical stance towards contemporary society. His style of writing, which was intended to create uncertainty and agitation in an audience, came to be known as the **Verfremdungseffekt** (alienation effect). Later successes included *Der gute Mensch von Sezuan* (*The Good Person of Sezuan*, 1943) which similarly showed an individual at odds with society. Probably his best known work was the play *Der kaukasische Kreidekreis* (*The Caucasian Chalk Circle*, first English performance 1948, German premiere 1954). Here Brecht examines motifs of social justice and the permanence of human relationships. At the core of the play is the claim of two women, Grusche and the governor's wife, to be allowed to raise a young baby. The chalk circle (taken from an ancient Chinese myth) is used by the judge Azdak to determine who should care for the child. Grusche refuses to take part in the experiment for fear of harming the child, and is promptly granted custody of him. This act, in turn, heralds a '**kurze, goldene Zeit beinahe der Gerechtigkeit**' ('short, golden period of near justice'), which had been conspicuously absent previously.

In the midst of the Expressionist movement one work stands out as exemplary. Alfred Döblin's **Großstadtroman** (novel of the city), *Berlin Alexanderplatz* (1929), was heavily influenced by John Dos Passos' *Manhattan Transfer* and James Joyce's *Ulysses*, and stands as the finest example of the late Expressionist movement known in Germany as **Neue Sachlichkeit** (New Objectivity). Döblin creates a literary montage of newspaper cuttings, lyrics from popular songs, advertising slogans and virtually any other text, in-between passages by the narrator, to relate the struggle of ex-convict Fritz Biberkopf to go straight after his release from prison. That Fritz cannot achieve his aim is seen as natural, even matter of fact, and he is merely a small part of the city which doesn't concern itself with the fate of one insignificant individual.

Literature in the Weimar Republic

The years after the First World War saw a thriving market for **Kriegserlebnisliteratur** (literature recounting experiences of the war) which seemed to show that the German people were not, after all, fed up of militarism. Ernst Jünger (born 1895), in *In Stahlgewittern* (*Storms of Steel*, 1920) does show the horrific life endured by men at the front, but at the same time glorifies the ability of the war to turn boys into men ... if they survived at all. Just a few years later Jünger was being hailed by the Nazis as a great National Socialist writer (something which he strongly denied after the war). Erich Maria Remarque, on the other hand, responded with his powerful anti-war novel *Im Westen nichts Neues* (*All Quiet on the Western Front*, 1929), which highlighted the appalling waste of young men's lives. Not surprisingly, the Nazis banned this war novel.

In the shadow of the swastika

State control: the *Reichsschrifttumskammer*

The decline of the Weimar Republic and the rise of the Nazis had a profound effect upon German literature, not all of it bad. We have already mentioned *In Stahlgewittern*, but as the German people forgot about the horrors of the First World War, so they turned more and more to right-wing fiction. Hans Grimm's *Volk ohne Raum* (*A People without Room*, 1926) first coined the phrase **Lebensraum** (space or room to live), which became a central tenet of the Nazis' expansionism. Needless to say, Grimm, Jünger and others quickly found favour under the Nazis, but those who did not saw their works condemned to the infamous night of bonfires on 10 May 1933, when Hitler Youth and students burned all books deemed **entartet** (degenerate) by Hitler. To ensure control of the work produced, the Nazis created an office to grant licences to authors, known as the **Reichsschrifttumskammer** (Reich Authors' Guild). Many authors were deported to labour camps, many committed suicide, and a large number, such as Bert Brecht, were forced into exile.

Schlüsselromane and inner emigration

Of course some authors chose to stay in Germany, choosing 'inner emigration' over foreign exile. They had to be careful to write books which did not invoke the wrath of the party. Some of these were actually cleverly coded stories of opposition, which managed to get past the censors because they seemed quite innocent on the surface. They were known as **Schlüsselromane** (key novels), implying that the reader needed the key to 'unlock' the hidden message. A great many were set in historical times, thus avoiding accusations of relevance to the current political situation. Werner Bergengruen published *Der Großtyrann und das Gericht* (*The Grand Tyrant and the Court*, 1935), which can be read as an attack on dictatorships, but which was so cleverly written that it was even published as a German Army field edition in 1941.

Post-war literature

Stunde Null

The period immediately after the defeat of Hitler's army was dubbed the **Stunde Null**, or Zero Hour. Many new and established authors saw this as an opportunity to rid the German language of its associations with National Socialism and wrote fiction and poetry about their war experiences in a cold, objective tone. One young man showed particular promise: Wolfgang Borchert (1921–1947) articulated all these feelings in his successful play *Draußen vor der Tür* (*Outside the Front Door*, 1947), but, tragically, he died as a result of diptheria contracted as a soldier on the Eastern Front. His play, however, stands as an important first step in the process of **Vergangenheitsbewältigung** (coming to terms with the past) which dominated German literature, and society, well into the 1960s.

Gruppe 47

A small group of authors decided to elevate **Vergangenheitsbewältigung** to the status of a literary programme. Hans Werner Richter and Alfred Andersch called these young authors together and founded the **Gruppe 47** (Group 47), which met for the first time on 10 September 1947. Wolfdietrich Schnurre opened the inaugural meeting with a public reading of a story called '*Das Begräbnis*' (*The Burial*), which suggested that God was dead following the events of the war. Some of the best literature produced in West Germany for the next two decades originated in the **Gruppe 47**. Andersch enjoyed success with novels such as *Die Kirschen der Freiheit* (*The Cherries of Freedom*, 1952) and *Sansibar oder der* *letzte Grund* (*Sansibar or the Final Reason*, 1957), which put forward existential ideas of choice, and the chance to start afresh. One of the early members was Heinrich Böll (1917–1985), a German author of international standing, who first came to the public eye in 1949 with *Der Zug war pünktlich* (*The Train was On Time*) and *Wo warst du, Adam?* (*Where were you, Adam?*, 1951). Böll is still considered by many to be Germany's greatest post-war author. His early works did much to help his country to explore the feelings of guilt, anger and regret brought on by wartime experiences. His central characters were generally anonymous young men, caught up in the horrors of war, who found themselves in the unenviable position of being **Mitläufer** (which translates as 'collaborators', but literally means 'people who run in the same direction') in the odious regime. Equally important is that Böll successfully gauged the swing in the population's mood as the 1950s wore on, and changed his style accordingly. The short novel *Die verlorene Ehre der Katharina Blum* (*The Lost Honour of Katharina Blum*, 1974) was a study of terrorism in 1970's Germany, but also a scathing attack on the liberties taken by the media in invading the life of the heroine, when she is suspected of harbouring a notorious RAF terrorist leader.

But of all the authors to emerge in the post-war period, particular mention must be made of Günter Grass. Born in 1927, Grass was younger than many of his **Gruppe 47** contemporaries, having served only as a boy anti-aircraft gunner in the final days of the war. His most famous literary creation, Oskar Matzerath, was also too young to play an active role in the war, but, crucially, this was because Oskar made a conscious decision to stop growing when he realised the terrible truth about the Nazis. The novel which features Oskar, *Die Blechtrommel* (*The Tin Drum*, 1959) has become the most successful German novel yet, selling worldwide in massive numbers. Grass has, along with Böll, continued to dominate the literary scene in Germany, even lending his weight to political campaigns at times, but has probably never enjoyed the levels of success of *Die Blechtrommel* again.

Classics of German literature 4: *Die Blechtrommel*, by Günter Grass

Grass's first novel, published in 1959, was an instant sensation. Based on some of his own experiences, and forming the first of what became the *Danziger Trilogie* (*Danzig Trilogy*), *Blechtrommel* was (at times) a painfully clear portrayal of the years before and during the Second World War. Seen from the viewpoint of Oskar Matzerath, a young boy who chooses not to grow, rather than become an adult in a disturbing world, the novel is supposedly written from the cell of an asylum for psychologically disturbed individuals, some years after the war. The novel begins with Oskar's grandmother, Anna Bronski, concealing her future husband under her flowing skirts when he is chased by the police. It then follows Oskar's birth and childhood, accompanied by his tin drum, which symbolises his resistance to the adult world in general, and the Nazi regime in particular. Drawing heavily on Döblin's style, Grass intermixes a wide range of images and word plays to create Germany's most successful novel of **Vergangenheitsbewältigung**. The novel was filmed by Volker Schlöndorff in 1978.

Short stories

One of the most successful forms of writing in the immediate post-war period was the **Kurzgeschichte** (short story). Modelling themselves on the American authors of the 1920s and 1930s, such as Hemingway and Steinbeck, the Germans who returned from the war found that this brusque style suited their need to express themselves simply. Early best-sellers were Böll's collection of stories *Wanderer, kommst du nach Spa...* (*Stranger, Bear Word to the Spartans, we...*, 1950) and one by Wolfdietrich Schnurre, entitled *Die Rohrdommel ruft jeden Tag* (*The Bittern calls Every Day*, 1950). Indeed, Schnurre became best known as a writer of short stories, studied by schoolchildren as part of their German literature courses. The title of another of his collections, *Man sollte dagegen sein* (*One Should have been Against It*, 1960) reveals the guilt which these authors, and others, were desperately trying to purge.

Recovery and rehabilitation

As conditions in Germany slowly improved, so the tone of the literature being written by West German authors also changed. Wolfgang Koeppen's first novel *Tauben im Gras* (*Pigeons in the Grass*, 1951) was a brilliant montage of interconnected lives in post-war Munich. Instead of looking back to the war, he looked towards the future, significantly making great play of the interaction between the Germans and their American occupiers.

Likewise, writers such as Siegfried Lenz and Peter Schneider continued the process of taking Germany beyond the war. First of all, however, they had to deal with the fact that a new generation of Germans was now questioning what their elders had done in the war, and criticising the society which had developed in the 1960s and 1970s. So, although Lenz's 1968 novel *Deutschstunde* (*German Lesson*) cannot be called a post-war novel, the fact that the central character writes an essay about his father's war shows that, in some ways, Germany was still far from rehabilitated.

East German literature

We must not forget, at this point, that there were two kinds of German literature in the post-war period, because there were two Germanies. In the Democratic Republic, authors were encouraged to adopt the Soviet literary style known as Socialist Realism. Whether they actually chose to follow this prescribed literary style, or in actual fact only paid lip-service to the state within which they lived, is one of the reasons why East German literature, which was largely ignored by West Germans during the Cold War, is worthy of greater attention.

East German *Vergangenheitsbewältigung*

In the East, just as in the West, the first priority was to come to terms with the immediate past. East Germany, in contrast to the West, was lucky to have many authors, expelled or in voluntary exile between 1933–1945, who chose to return to the East because of their Socialist or Communist sympathies (interestingly, far fewer exiles chose to return to the West). Notable among these were Bert

Brecht and Anna Seghers (1900–1983), who in exile had already published an account of life in a Nazi labour camp, called *Das siebte Kreuz* (*The Seventh Cross*). In 1947 she was awarded the Georg-Büchner-Preis, the top literary prize in Germany, in recognition of her work.

Some of the East German literary stars produced work every bit the equal of the best the West could offer. Christa Wolf (born 1929) first enjoyed acclaim with her critical novel *Der geteilte Himmel* (*The Divided Sky*), in 1963. The novel outlines the frustrations of a young woman, Rita Seidel, who has suffered a nervous breakdown in the summer of 1961: it was one of the first works in the East to deal with the construction of the Wall and certainly contained a critique of the East German regime, as did most of Wolf's works. Ironically, however, many observers in the West accused Wolf of failing to criticise enough, but she, like her colleagues, knew that there was a fine line between what the East German authorities would tolerate and what they would not.

Other notable successes in the East came from Ulrich Plenzdorf (born 1934), who paralled Goethe's famous story in *Die Neuen Leiden des jungen W* (*The New Sorrows of the Young W*, 1973). Günter de Bruyn (born 1926) took a swipe at the bureaucracy and petty-mindedness of the East German system in *Märkische Forschungen* (*Marcher Researches*, 1979).

Literature of reunified Germany

It is not surprising that the events of 1989 had their effect on literature, just as they affected every other aspect of German life. It was Peter Schneider who commented in his 1984 book *Der Mauerspringer* (*The Wall Jumper*) that East German writers at least had the advantage that the authorities took their literature seriously: they read it very closely for every critical phrase and sometimes acted to censure an author who became too critical. In fact, some authors who became too critical had been **ausgebürgert** (their citizenship was revoked) over the years, creating a small, but influential, group of ex-GDR writers in the West.

Now, however, the Wall was down and the literary playing field was level. In *Der Mauerspringer* Schneider had prophetically warned that '**Die Mauer im Kopf einzureißen wird länger dauern, als irgendein Abrißunternehmen für die sichtbare Mauer**' ('It will take longer to tear down the wall in the head, than any demolition job on the visible wall'). Although Erich Loest enthusiastically portrayed the events leading up to the **Wende** in his novel *Nikolaikirche* (*Nikolai Church*), the disappointment of the East German population at large was apparent in Christa Wolf's *Was bleibt?* (*What's left?*, 1990). This was an attempt to take stock of the historical events of unification which, perhaps inevitably, contained a hint of regret at losing some of the good things to come out of the GDR. The novel sparked off great controversy in the German press, not least because it transpired that Wolf had, like countless other East Germans, been recruited by the East German secret service, the Stasi, to act as an **inoffizieller Mitarbeiter** (IM, an unofficial informant). It was a period of bitterness and recrimination in Germany, reflecting the upheavals of 1945 in many ways; it has quietened in recent years, but not gone away altogether.

Contemporary literature

And what of the contemporary literary scene in Germany? Although it is always difficult to predict which books of one's own time will go on to count as classics, some new writers have hit the scene in recent years. The Bavarian Herbert Rosendorfer enjoyed modest success with titles such as *Die Nacht der Amazonen* (*The Night of the Amazons*) and *Briefe aus der chinesischen Vergangenheit* (*Letters from the Chinese Past*) in the 1980s. Patrick Süskind has written a string of bestsellers in the 1980s and 1990s, with his best success perhaps being *Parfüm* (*Perfume*, 1985). This is the bizarre story of a Parisian loner with a phenomenal sense of smell, who turns to murder to experience new smells and to capture the essence of human smell. It is worth noting that this novel also broke onto the international scene, signalling a new, wider appreciation of German literature in recent years. More recently, for instance, Bernhard Schlink sold over 1 million copies of his novel **Der Vorleser** (*The Reader*, 1995) in the USA. Similarly, the 1999 recipient of the Büchner-Preis, Arnold Stadler, has enjoyed a wider commercial success than many of his prize-winning predecessors.

Finally, several names from the past continue to publish and to achieve respectable sales. Günter de Bruyn has, alongside Christa Wolf, gone on to be a most successful ex-GDR author. His autobiographical work **Zwischenbilanz** (*Interim Balance*, 1992) went to three prints in its first year of publication. Günter Grass, too, has been a prolific writer throughout his career. **Ein weites Feld** (*A Wide Field*, 1995) was a controversial examination of German-Polish relations, while his most recent work **Mein Jahrhundert** (*My Century*, 1999), a review of German history in the 20th century, was still in the German top 10 fiction chart in October 1999, many weeks after its publication. Whatever the response to his recent work, the award of the Nobel Prize for Literature in December 1999 underlined Grass's standing as a major figure in European literature. With the prospect of these and other contemporary German authors gaining more and more recognition in translation, the state of German literature at the beginning of the 21st century is as healthy as it has ever been.

GLOSSARY

die Literatur *literature*
der Autor (-en) / die Autorin (-nen) *author*
der Dichter (-) / die Dichterin (-nen) *poet*
das Buch (¨-er) *book*
der Roman (-e) *novel*

das Schauspiel (-e) *play*
die Philosophie *philosophy*
der Philosoph (-en) / die Philosphin (-nen) *philosopher*
schreiben *to write*
lesen *to read*

Taking it further

You might be surprised at how accessible many of the great German authors are to read. This is true even if you decide to have a go at reading them in the original version, but in the following list of recommended reading, information about English translations has been included wherever possible. You could start with a parallel text, where the German original is on one page with an

English translation placed opposite. Or you could find one of the many abridged and annotated versions available for students, before tackling 'the real thing'. Finally, when reading a German play or novel, try not to get bogged down by looking up every new word in a dictionary: you don't necessarily know every English word you read in a book, so allow the context to help you understand. Get into the habit of reading fluently, for pleasure, even if some passages are too difficult for you ... it will pay off in the long term.

I ought to stress at this point that this list is only the tip of the iceberg and is my recommendation only. Also, I have deliberately concentrated largely on works published in the last 100 years, because each will give you a useful insight into the lifestyle and culture of the German people today. Hopefully you will then be inspired to delve deeper into the canon of German literature of previous centuries.

Reading

Goethe, *Faust*. Considered by many to be *the* German classic, and a chilling premonition of Germany's pact with the devil in the 20th century. Available from Oxford University Press, ISBN 0-19-283595-5.

Brecht, *Die Dreigroschenoper*. Another of Brecht's masterpieces, this was one of his earlier successes. Available in English as *The Threepenny Opera* from Methuen, ISBN 0-41-339030-6.

Remarque, *Im Westen nichts Neues*. Classic anti-war novel, available as *All Quiet on the Western Front*, Vintage Books, ISBN 0-09953281-6.

Kafka, *Der Prozeß*. Complete with long corridors and 'kafkaesque' confusion. Available as *The Trial*, Penguin, ISBN 0-14-018622-0.

Mann, *Buddenbrooks*. An epic account of four generations of one family in Lübeck, up to the start of the 20th century. Published in English by Minerva, ISBN 0-74-938647-9.

Grass, *Die Blechtrommel*. Compelling account of Nazism in Danzig. Available in English as *The Tin Drum*, Vintage Books, ISBN 0-67972575-X.

Böll, *Erzählungen*. Many collections of Böll's stories are available in German and English. An easy first text in German, perhaps, because some stories are only two or three pages long.

Wolf, *Der geteilte Himmel*. Interesting account of life in East Germany.

Loest, *Nikolaikirche*. Portrays events leading up to reunification from the perspective of the ordinary people.

Süskind, *Parfüm*. Gripping novel from one of Germany's top contemporary authors. Part historical, part crime story, part psychological profile. Published in English as *Perfume*, by Penguin, ISBN 0-14012083-1.

4 ART AND ARCHITECTURE

Caspar David Friedrich, the Brandenburg Gate, Albrecht Dürer, Neuschwanstein Castle: Germany has long been considered a country of great architectural and artistic achievement. Admittedly, it has rarely been at the forefront of artistic developments, but it has certainly always enthusiastically embraced the various European styles, and not infrequently has gone on to offer particularly fine examples of these styles. Interestingly, German art and architecture has always been characterised by an important spiritual element, searching for what the Germans call '**das Wesentliche**' (the essential).

Of course, many of Germany's great buildings are now an amalgamation of several styles and artistic developments: work on Cologne Cathedral lasted some 600 years, only finishing in the 1880s. Many important buildings, paintings, statues and other works of art were destroyed either wilfully at the hands of the Nazis in the early 1930s, or as a result of the Allied bombings of Germany in 1944 and 1945. Luckily a great deal survived, both of the buildings and of the artistic treasures that were housed in them. The aim of this chapter is to take you on a quick walk through the most important of them.

Pre-8th century: Roman remains

Relatively little has survived from the Roman period to the present day. The legacy of the Romans can be best seen in Trier, where remains of the **Kaiserthermen** (imperial baths), the Amphitheatre and, best preserved, the massive Porta Nigra gate – the largest in the Roman Empire – all bear testimony to the importance of this city in the Roman period. Equally impressive is the huge basilica, now the Protestant parish church, which was built in the 3rd century and rivals even the Pantheon in Rome as a masterpiece of Roman engineering and construction. Lesser remains can be seen around the country, for instance the Roman Wall sections of Mainz, and the line of the *limes* (see Chapter 1) can be traced right along the Romano-German border thanks to the many remnants of the small border forts which held the barbarians at bay for so long. One fort, the Saalburg, near Bad Homburg in Hessen, was reconstructed earlier this century and is particularly interesting to visit.

8th–10th centuries: Early period

Carolingian architecture

Our knowledge of the customs, the art and the architecture of the early Germans is rather limited. We have to look ahead to the reign of Charlemagne (768–814) to see the development of a truly Germanic style of art and architecture. This period, known as the Carolingian, saw attempts to recreate the pomp and grandeur of the ancient Roman buildings, not least in a whole series of cathedrals across the empire. The abbey church at Fulda, where construction began in 791, was commissioned to be built in the *more romano* (the Roman way), which meant an imitation of the Christian edifices in Rome itself. The remains of St Boniface, who played an important role in bringing Christianity to the Germanic tribes, were interred there in 819, and the present cathedral is the result of extensive work in the 18th century. The Palatine Chapel in Aachen (completed 805), the northern capital of Charlemagne's empire, was likewise a close copy of the basilica of San Vitale in Ravenna. It was built to demonstrate that Charlemagne was a worthy successor to the Roman Emperors, and his imperial throne can still be seen there, as can his tomb, dating from his beatification in 1165.

Ottonian period

The efforts of Charlemagne were continued by the Saxon Ottonian rulers who inherited his empire in the 900s. The first Otto founded the German Holy Roman Empire and immediately set about an even more ambitious building programme, founding the cathedrals of Magdeburg (construction begun in 955), Münster (967), Mainz (975), Hildesheim (1001) and Merseburg (1015). This apparent generosity was not just out of piety, however, but also to gain the support of the powerful bishops!

Mainz Cathedral: Testament to the Power of the Church

At the time of the Ottonian kings the Church was a serious threat to the authority of the court. Like several others Mainz Cathedral was built to underline the authority of Archbishop Willigis, with work beginning in 975. The greatest phase of construction, however, took place long after Willigis's death, in the mid- to late-1200s. The **Dom St Martin und St Stephan**, to give the cathedral its full title, boasts six fine towers and a vast nave. Standing in the **Stephansplatz** in central Mainz, it is an imposing sight. Architectural styles and artistic works from virtually every period in Germany's history can be found here, right up to modern stained glass designed by Marc Chagall.

Artistic developments

At the same time, jewellery making and gold working were flourishing in the German cities, while the illustration of Christian manuscripts became a major part of the work in monasteries, such as the lavishly illustrated *Codex Egberti* in Trier, or the *Gospels of Otto III*, produced at Reichenau in about 1000. Sculpture, too, began to decorate churches and cathedrals.

11th century: Romanesque

Despite the name 'Romanesque' to describe the work produced in the 11th century, this new period established a truly German artistic style for the first time. Stone became the staple medium for building, not only to continue the Ottonian love of huge soaring cathedrals but also to create more permanent public buildings too. Trends first seen in the later Ottonian cathedrals, of large vaults, majestic semi-circular arches, geometric naves and imposing double towers, developed into the Romanesque edifices of the cathedrals at Speyer (begun 1030) and Goslar (1050). Frescoes began to decorate the interiors of these churches, illustrating stories from the Bible to teach the illiterate. Later, new buildings – such as the cathedrals at Worms (1100) and Bamberg (1205) – and ongoing work on existing buildings showed increasingly daring vault-work and a greater use of sculpture to accompany the painted frescoes.

A quick guide to Romanesque architecture

Look for a blocky style of construction, with large square towers. You will also notice round-topped arcades, windows and doorways.

Religious art

Art in this time was still almost entirely religious in nature. The reputation of German metalwork continued in several of the booming cities. Although jewellery making also flourished still, the work produced in workshops such as that of Nicholas of Verdun established a Europe-wide reputation for fine detail and great beauty. The altar at Klosterneuburg Altar (1181) and the Shrine of the Three Kings (1196), which can be seen at Cologne Cathedral, are considered superb examples of applied art from this period.

13th century: Gothic

Architecture

In the 13th century the styles and techniques of Germany's builders continued to develop in new and daring directions. The period came to define the Gothic style, initially meant as a derisive term referring to the barbarian (i.e. non-Roman) style. It all came about because of the rapid growth of the German towns and the rise of the middle class **Bürger** (burgher, or citizen), who had newly earned wealth to spend on worldly items and activities. New techniques in construction allowed truly breathtaking innovations: towers and spires reached for the heavens, arches soared upwards to meet in impossibly sharp points, flying buttresses allowed vast **Hallenkirchen** (hall churches with huge rectangular naves), such as the **Liebfrauenkirche** in Munich (1468). Delicate tracery and stained glass also began to add even greater beauty to the buildings. Around 1250 work began on the **Dom** (cathedral) in Cologne, incorporating many of these innovations, but this great work of pious devotion was not to be completed until half a millennium later! In the north, the use of red brick, rather than cut stone, became common at this time, notably in the **Marienkirche** in Lübeck (1291). All these architectural features were, of course, dedicated to God, but significantly they were designed to show man's wealth and talents also.

The *Dom zu Köln*: six hundred years of devotion to God

The story of Cologne Cathedral is quite remarkable. A church had stood on the site of the cathedral for several hundred years when, during the reign of Friedrich Barbarossa (1152–1197), it was decided to build a new cathedral to reflect the importance of the city as a centre of pilgrimage. The foundation stone was laid in 1248 and the choir was the first part of the cathedral to be consecrated in 1322. Work continued apace, this time on the transept, but ground to a halt in 1559, leaving various parts of the building only half-finished, including the south tower. Walls were simply concreted up at whatever point they had reached, and the crane on the incomplete tower loomed high over the city for the next few centuries!

Eventually a wave of enthusiasm for all things medieval in the Romantic period of the 19th century saw work begin again. On 15 October 1880 the amazing edifice was finally consecrated in the presence of Kaiser Wilhelm I. Less than a hundred years later, during severe Allied bombing of the city centre, it seemed certain that the building would be flattened. But, miraculously, it stood proud throughout the most horrific bombing, until every other building within sight had been razed to the ground. Today it contains many important treasures, including the Reliquary of the Three Kings, said to contain the bones of the Wise Men who visited the baby Jesus, and the cause of Cologne's fame when they were brought to the site of the cathedral in 1181.

A quick guide to Gothic architecture

In this era, technological advances allowed daring new designs, with tall spires, large rosette windows and fine tracery predominating. Inside, vaulted arches span seemingly impossible distances.

Sculpture

Stone carving at this time was initially still a rather crude affair, known as the **Zackenstil** (jagged style). Only later did German sculpture begin to soften: clothing, for example, began to be represented as free-flowing material in its own right, as opposed to earlier, cruder representations which clung to the bodies of the sculptures. This 'soft style' was pioneered by sculptors of the **Kölner Schule** (Cologne School) such as Meister Francke and Konrad von Soest, or the wood carvings of Tilman Riemenschneider (1460–1531), whose work includes several remarkable altarpieces in Würzburg and south-west Germany.

Painting

For the most part, paintings at the start of the Gothic period were still purely religious, commissioned by bishops or benefactors. Gradually it began to develop into an art form in its own right. Meister Bertram (ca.1345–1415), for instance, is the first artist known to have painted narrative cycles on small panels. Nearly a century later, Hans Pleydenwurff (ca.1420–72), began to paint naturalist scenes in the background of his work. Here, too, we talk of the **Kölner Schule**, where artists were developing a more realistic and softer technique for portraying the world around them. Although technically still a religious picture, Stefan Lochner's (ca.1410–51) *Dombild* (literally: cathedral painting), a triptych (three-panelled painting) of the Epiphany with representations of Cologne's patron saints, is one of the best examples of this. In it we see much fine detail, realistic postures and groupings, and careful shading, as well as a more dynamic narrative style. This late Gothic Realism was also represented by Lukas Moser (painting around 1430) and particularly Konrad Witz (ca.1400–1450), a Swiss Realist, whose *Christ Walking on Water* (1444) boasts the earliest recognisable scene of a real location – Lake Geneva – in European art.

15th century: Renaissance

The influence of the Italian Renaissance reached Germany very early because of the busy trade which went on between the great Italian cities of Venice and Florence, for instance, and the southern German centres of Munich, Basle and Nuremberg. One of the main features of Renaissance art in Germany, however, is that different artists, sculptors, painters and so on interpreted the humanist ideals of the movement in different ways: no one style or feature can be said to be 'the German Renaissance', but rather it is the blossoming of art during these years which makes the period stand out.

Martin Schongauer: The father of the German Renaissance

One of the first to import the Italian ideas was Martin Schongauer (ca.1450–1490), whom many consider the father of Renaissance art in Germany. His *Madonna of the Rosehedge* (1473) can be seen in Colmar, and displays the bold new style of artists from this time. He was also an engraver of some repute, and one story tells that Albrecht Dürer, the other great exponent of the Renaissance in Germany, travelled for many days to meet the master, only to be told that Schongauer had died while he was journeying.

Albrecht Dürer: Renaissance man

But it is the same Albrecht Dürer (1471–1528) who is generally acknowledged as the greatest of Germany's Renaissance artists, and the first to make an impact on European and world art. He studied his art under Meister Michael Wolgemut (1434–1519) in Nuremberg, then travelled to Italy to study. By 1512 he was court painter to Emperor Maximilian and had achieved great fame and wealth. As well as a number of woodcut series, such as *Apocalypse* (1498), engravings – *Prodigal Son* (1497) and *The Knight, Death and the Devil* (1513) – book illustrations and even watercolours, he also published books on subjects as varied as siege warfare, artistic theory and travel. He was a true Renaissance man, in the mould of Leonardo da Vinci (whom Dürer greatly admired from his trips to Italy), and introduced to Germany the notion that a man of education could be a scholar in many disciplines, rather than be restricted to that of his training.

The Danube School

A little later still, Albrecht Altdorfer (ca.1480–1538), a Bavarian who worked in Regensburg, virtually created the **Donauer Schule** (Danube School). He and his followers came to enjoy a reputation for great landscapes – the first pure landscape painting in Europe to be free of religious overtones, such as his *Danube Landscape* (1520) of the great river near Regensburg.

Lucas Cranach the Elder (1472–1553) became famous for work with a humanist touch, particularly his nudes. In 1505 he moved to Wittenberg and became a great friend of Martin Luther, whom he painted. In fact, it is thought that Cranach was the first artist to paint full-length portraits.

Finally, Hans Holbein the Elder (1465–1524) established a workshop in Augsburg in the early 1500s. His work was rather more late Gothic than Renaissance, but his son, Hans Holbein the Younger (1497–1543) went on to become another great Renaissance artist. His realistic portraits were in great demand, with one of the European scholar Erasmus (1523) being particularly well known, and he finished his life in London as court painter to Henry VIII. His work was renowned for being a rich mix of traditional motifs with contemporary scenes, such as the *Dance of Death* (1523) and *Alphabet of Death* (1524).

Architecture and sculpture

The period of the Renaissance in Germany saw very few developments in the fields of the applied arts and architecture. In Nuremberg, Peter Vischer the Elder was producing bronze work of great note which drew inspiration from the monumental statuary of the Italian sculptors. He created a series of statues for the tomb of Maximilian I in Innsbruck, when the Emperor died in 1550.

17th and 18th centuries: Baroque and Rococo

If the Renaissance period was largely seen in the works of the fine arts, developments in the 17th and 18th centuries were limited almost exclusively to the realm of architecture and interior design. After the misery of the Thirty Years' War this period was bursting with a new optimism, resulting in great architectural innovations. Although there was a definite split between the different regions of Germany (particularly between north and south, which looked to the Netherlands and to Italy respectively for inspiration), sweeping staircases, vast stuccoed ceilings with *trompe l'oeil* (paintings with false perspectives and optical illusions), visual effects and masses of gilded plaster characterised many of the best Baroque and Rococo buildings. Indeed, for many visitors to Germany it is the architecture of this period which seems most typically part of

A quick guide to Baroque architecture

Heavily influenced by the Italian Renaissance, Baroque architecture is a riot of columns, stairways and domes. Interiors are further decorated with lavish gilt coverings and stuccoed plaster ceilings.

Germany's cultural heritage, particularly in Berlin and Dresden in the east, and the southern cities of Munich and Würzburg.

The Dresden *Zwinger*: Post-GDR restoration

Like many of Germany's national architectural treasures, the Baroque splendour of the **Zwinger** found itself behind the Iron Curtain after the construction of the **Mauer** in 1961. And, like many of these treasures, it was long neglected. Along with the **Jungfrauenkirche** which was all but destroyed during the RAF's infamous firebombing of the city, these buildings are symbolic of the struggles faced by a reunited Germany to preserve her heritage. Almost as soon as the party for reunification was over, the **Zwinger** was covered in kilometres of green protective sheeting as restoration work began ... at times, it seemed as if the whole of the former GDR was under such sheeting. The project to restore the **Jungfrauenkirche** is a little trickier, however, because it will require millions of Marks, and although a public campaign to raise the necessary funds began in the late 1990s, it is likely to be many years before restoration is complete.

In Berlin, the **Kurfürst** (Elector) Friedrich I began work on the **Schloß Charlottenburg** (1695–1707). In Dresden, Matthäus Poppelmann constructed the **Zwinger**, a park-cum-courtyard in the centre of the Dresden Palace surrounded by colonnades and sculptures, in 1711.

Meanwhile in the south, Johann Balthasar Neumann (1687–1753) began work on the Würzburg **Residenz** in 1719, which boasted fantastic sweeping staircases, while the Asam brothers, Egid (1692–1750) and Cosmas (1686–1739), decorated Munich churches in ornate gilded designs and riots of stucco, most famously the **Asamkirche** in the centre of the city. Outside the city, the Bavarian court architect François Cuvilliés built the Amalienburg Pavilion in the **Schloß Nymphenburg**. Finally, another pair of brothers, architect Dominikus Zimmermann (1685–1766) and fresco-painting brother Johann Baptist (1680–1785) became two of the most celebrated protagonists of the Baroque period, with the Bavarian pilgrimage chapel, the **Wieskirche** ('Meadow Church', 1750) being one of their best-known creations.

Artistic developments

Although we have already said that architecture was foremost among the arts in this period, the paintings of Adam Elsheimer were very popular. Like Altdorfer before him, Elsheimer produced landscapes of great merit (e.g. *Flight to Egypt*, 1609). The first European porcelain factory was opened in 1710, in Mainz. This art form went on to enjoy particular success in Germany, with the figurines produced at Meissen in Saxony becoming collectors' pieces around the world.

18th century: Neoklassik

The rise of Berlin

The end of the 18th century saw the rise of the Prussians as the Hohenzollern family strove to improve the country's standing. An ambitious building programme was begun by the **Großer Kurfürst** (Great Elector) Friedrich I, who intended to turn Berlin into a city of international standing with a beauty and grandeur to rival that of Versailles, London or Venice. At the same time, the discovery and first excavations of the buried city of Pompeii in 1748 released a wave of enthusiasm for the simple symmetry and Doric columns of the ancients. Johann Winckelmann (1717–1768), a distinguished art historian of the day, gave added impetus to this **Neoklassik** (Neo-classicism) when he published *Gedanken über die Nachahmung der griechischen Werke* (*Thoughts Regarding the Imitation of Greek Works*, 1755). In it, he calls for '**edle Einfalt und stille Größe**' ('noble simplicity and quiet greatness'), and it was this that Friedrich and his successors wanted for Berlin.

In 1791 the **Brandenburger Tor** (Brandenburg Gate) was completed, to stand squarely across the main thoroughfare through Berlin. Capped by Quadriga – the goddess of victory – in her chariot, it (and the **Siegessäule**, or Victory Column, erected some 80 years later, facing the Gate) was intended as a symbol of Prussia's military strength.

But the building did not stop there. Karl-Friedrich Schinkel (1781–1841) was the man who was called upon to mastermind much of Berlin's building. A walk through the city quickly reveals the extent of the programme he undertook. The famous street

The *Brandenburger Tor*: Symbol of a nation

For many, the Brandenburg Gate represents not just Prussia, but Germany as a whole. Over the years the Gate has been a silent witness to many of the greatest events of German history: Napoleon marched his troops through it as he headed for his disastrous Russian winter campaign against Moscow; the Russians flew the Communist flag from the Quadriga as the city fell in 1945; they then built a wall which ran virtually through the Gate in 1961 to divide the city – and the country – in two. Most recently, the Gate was the focal point of the huge party when the Wall fell in 1989 and when Germany was formally reunited in November 1990.

Unter den Linden has Schinkel to thank for its current appearance, as it runs east from the Brandenburg Gate. As you continue to walk you reach the **Platz der Akademie** (Academy Square), dominated by the **Schauspielhaus** (theatre) and the German and French Churches (the latter built to accommodate the French Huguenots, whom Friedrich had sheltered during their persecution in France). Then there is the so-called **Museumsinsel** (Museum Island) standing in the middle of the River Spree, which is the location of several majestic, collonaded museums and galleries, including the Pergamon Museum.

Outside Berlin, the Royal Palace of Potsdam had been growing in stature from its origins in 1660. It was first developed by the architect Knobelsdorff in 1745, to turn Sans Souci into a military garrison for Friedrich's honour guard and also a centre of culture and pleasure to rival the French royal palace of Versailles. Schinkel then completed the transformation, building the orangery and the spectacular flights of steps leading up to it, as well as having the gardens laid out in beautifully intricate patterns of paths, bushes, fountains and flower beds.

Neo-classical art

As well as building Neo-classical Berlin, Schinkel used his talents to paint painstakingly detailed scenes of Berlin in the late 18th century. They were almost coloured architectural drawings, so accurate were they, but they lacked a warmth which was only to come as Schinkel embraced the Romantic movement of the early 19th century. At this time Johann Wilhelm Tischbein (1751–1829) was painting idyllic landscapes that idealised German life and ushered in the Romantic movement. It was Tischbein who painted a number of famous portraits of Goethe.

19th century: Romantik

As the 19th century dawned the rather cold realism of the **Neoklassik** started to be replaced by an idealised view of the past which was called **Neogotik** (Neo-Gothic) in its early days. It signified a revival of interest in Germany's medieval past which led, for instance, to the completion of Cologne cathedral. A number of artists, too, produced paintings of medieval idylls where elaborate fantasy castles or cathedrals watched over the bucolic lives of the simple people below. Schinkel, in particular, embraced this form of Romanticism with great enthusiasm.

Probably the most famous of the Romantics was Caspar David Friedrich (1774–1840). Born in Greifswald, on the northern German coast, Friedrich painted broad canvases of seemingly empty landscapes, Gothic ruins, stormy cliff scenes and moonlit shores where the humans are virtually incidental to the natural world. His painting *Der Wanderer über dem Nebelmeer* (*Wanderer above the Sea of Fog*, 1818) shows the ideal situation for a man of Friedrich's sensibilities, lost on a peak which is seemingly an island in the fog. A contemporary of Friedrich's, Philipp Otto Runge (1777–1810) produced work on different, but equally Romantic, lines. He painted many portraits of chubby children and equally chubby women, but his most famous painting is *Die Ruhe auf der Flucht* (*Rest during the Flight*, 1805), a highly stylised representation of the flight of the Holy Family into Egypt.

The *Nazarener*

The **Nazarener**, or Nazarenes, were a group of painters similar in style and approach to the Pre-Raphaelites in Britain. Founded by Johann Overbeck (1789–1869), and Peter Cornelius (1783–1867), the group experimented with medieval painting techniques, and many converted to Catholicism as part of their commitment to the movement. The allegorical painting *Italia und Germania* (1828) shows the two countries as female friends against a background full of references to Germany and Italy, as testimony to the close ties which this group felt with the southern country.

Romantic castles

Although there was little or no original development in architectural styles in Germany, the Romantics did have an effect here too, because of the fascination with the past. Many of the most spectacular castles along the Rhine, for instance, which might seem at first to be medieval, in fact date from this period, or are the product of extensive restoration. The fortress of **Schloß Stolzenfels**, for instance, located south of Koblenz, is a design of Karl Friedrich Schinkel built on earlier foundations.

But it is in Bavaria where the Romantic period saw its greatest architectural work. This is due to the fantastic wishes of the Bavarian kings Ludwig I and Ludwig II. The former was responsible for the **Walhalla** (Valhalla temple), at Donaustauf, designed along Greek lines to hold busts of the great Germans. It was built between 1830 and 1841 and initially contained busts of such Germans as Erasmus, Goethe, Luther and Wagner. It was Ludwig's son, Ludwig II, who had the fairy-tale castle of Neuschwanstein built in 1869. This astonishing work seems to be a cake decoration rather than a castle, so ornate and delicate is its tracery and its slender towers, but it has gone on to become one of the most photographed castles in the world, so Ludwig must have known what he was doing, mad or not!

Late 19th century: Biedermeier

In the rapid growth which accompanied Germany's relatively late development into an industrial power, the middle classes also quickly came to occupy a large niche in German society. The term **Biedermeier** (which comes from two fictitious dimwits called Biedermann and Bummelmeier) was used to describe the particularly heavy tastes of this group in art and interior design. Rather like similar developments in Victorian Britain, the decoration of the parlour and sitting room in houses in Wilhelminian Germany was regarded as a sign of the owner's (supposedly good) taste. Although we usually think of **Biedermeier** in terms of furniture, one artist at least has come to be considered the visual equivalent of the middle-class sitting room. The paintings of Karl Spitzweg (1808–1885) were in the style of cartoons, almost caricatures of the new social class. In a series of *Kakteenfreund* (*Cactus Lover*) paintings he fondly shows various bachelors besotted by their harmless, rather bourgeois hobby. *Engländer in der Campagna* (*Englishfolk in the Campagna*, 1835), by way of contrast, sends up the new practice of tourism. Spitzweg's best-loved picture, though, is *Der arme Poet* (*The Poor Poet*, 1839) which again pokes gentle fun at a scholarly man, trying to write his poetry in bed in his cramped, cold garret. Indeed, there is the suggestion that Spitzweg is actually mocking himself and his fellows in this and other paintings in the series.

The end of the 19th century: Sezession and Jugendstil

At the end of the 19th century some artists and designers began to rebel against the strict formality of the great academies, choosing to strike out and seek their own paths. The Berlin Secessionists, as these independents were called, were grouped around Max Liebermann (1847–1928). Liebermann had been one of the few Germans to be influenced by the French Impressionists, themselves considered anti-establishmentarian in their early days, and had struggled with a small group of like-minded German painters to reconcile the Impressionists' aims with the generally more spiritual approach of German art. More important were the Munich Secessionists, who coined the phrase **Jugendstil** (literally 'youth style', implying the vitality of the new movement) after the journal which was their mouthpiece in the 1890s. This group was centred on Franz von Stuck (1863–1928) and together with the Berliners, and the vitally important centre of the Viennese Secessionists (Gustav Klimt being the best known of the Austrians), they created a short-lived but hugely important movement which affected every aspect of applied and fine arts. Secession buildings of the highest quality can be seen in many German cities (notably Darmstadt, although Vienna and Prague are probably the most stunning), while furniture design created exciting, futuristic pieces which were still strictly functional (with parallels to the Glasgow School of Charles Rennie Mackintosh and Britain's other Arts and Crafts designers). In literature, as well as jewellery making, glass blowing, ceramics, metalworking and sculpture, artists found themselves liberated in a way which meant radical new designs and effectively paved the way for the first major artistic movement of the dawning 20th century: Expressionism.

Expressionism in art

The impact of Expressionism on German culture simply cannot be underestimated. We saw in Chapter 3 how this movement revolutionised German literature, but it was in architecture and the visual arts that it had its greatest impact. In Germany, Expressionism became particularly associated with the cities, but the first impetus came from abroad. Inspired by the French *fauves* movement, a number of German artists moved towards a unique brand of Expressionism. Two main groups evolved: **Die Brücke** and **Der Blaue Reiter**.

Die Brücke (*The Bridge*) was founded in 1905 in Dresden. As the name suggests, the group sought a way to bridge the gap (as they saw it) between art and the natural world, and subjective emotion. The main exponents of the group were Ernst Ludwig Kirchner (1880–1938), Erich Heckel (1883–1970) and Karl Schmidt-Rottluff (1884–1976). The group made bold experiments with colour in their early works and then, following a move to Berlin, with bright, busy city scenes.

At almost the same time, the group called **Der Blaue Reiter** (The Blue Rider) was founded in 1911 in Munich by Wassily Kandinsky (1866–1944) and Franz Marc (1880–1916). Their aim was similar to that of the **Brücke**: to promote the use of colour and experimentation with shape and form. The group took its name from a Kandinsky painting at one of the early exhibitions. It expanded slowly, and included notable Expressionist painters such as August Macke (1879–1940) and Paul Klee (1879–1940), who was Swiss, but spent his whole career living and working in Germany. Eventually the Blue Riders eclipsed the fame of the **Brücke** painters. Gradually the four leaders became more and more abstract, with the North African paintings of Macke and Klee showing signs of early Cubism, but the movement was cut short by the First World War.

The Expressionist period was particularly rich for artists. Independent of the groups already mentioned, many others were also producing work of some distinction. The key term to describe their efforts is **Neue Sachlichkeit** (New Objectivity). It refers to their attempts to portray their bewildering society with new, 'unromantic' techniques. The main artists of this style were Emil Nolde (1867–1956), who produced ugly, distorted paintings of the world around him. George Grosz (1893–1959) and Otto Dix (1891–1969) were drawn to the image of the big city. Using techniques such as montage they portrayed Berlin's seedy nightlife, its clubs and prostitutes. Käthe Kollwitz (1867–1945) specialised in woodcuts and engravings of working class life, then explored the theme of mother and son after the losses of the First World War. Finally, Ernst Barlach (1870–1938) became best known for his stark but emotive sculpture.

A quick guide to Bauhaus architecture

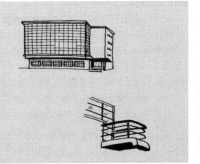

As the first 'modern' architectural style, Bauhaus makes much use of glass and steel. Look for combinations of straight lines, right angles and curves.

Bauhaus

The architectural style which was influenced by the Expressionist movement was known as **Bauhaus**. It took its name from the **Staatliches Bauhaus** (State Building School) in Weimar, which was run by Walter Gropius (1883–1969) from 1919. Its curriculum was heavily influenced by the British Arts and Crafts movement, with influential teachers like Kandinsky and Klee, but had a much more modern outlook. The angular designs, and use of glass and steel, mixed with traditional forms, produced a radical new style which swept the world.

In the shadow of the swastika

There is little to be said about art and architecture in Nazi Germany. The regime banned all artists and styles which did not suit their political aims, dismissing them as **entartet** (degenerate). Hitler and his followers preferred art which mimicked the Classic style, and celebrated what they saw as bucolic country lifestyles. If we talk at all of a Nazi 'style', then it is a style which many critics dismissively call **Blut und Boden** (Blood and Earth). Of more significance is that many of Germany's treasures, and those of countries invaded by the Nazis, were lost in the confusion and the destruction of the final days of the war.

Modern architecture

In the years immediately following the war the priority was to rebuild the shattered cities, and creative art was a luxury few could afford to indulge in. Gradually, however, as the country began to grow in confidence and wealth, stylish new buildings were built to grace the flourishing cities. Here, as elsewhere, there were significant differences between developments in the West and those in East Germany. Although they had inherited many buildings of worldwide significance, the East German authorities were forced to concentrate on the productivity of their factories, and the housing of the workers. So the architectural style of the East was dominated by new concrete buildings, and old decaying buildings, with little creativity to compensate. One spectacular exception to this rule was

A quick guide to post-war Architecture

Improved methods for producing steel, concrete and glass have allowed architects to reach new heights, and to flood the interiors of their creations with light.

the **Fernsehturm** (television tower) in East Berlin. It is a needle-thin tower capped by a large metallic sphere, containing a viewing gallery and revolving restaurant, which dominates the whole Berlin cityscape. Even in the days before the fall of the Wall the tower had become a landmark for both sides of the city.

If the cityscapes of East Germany were grey, the same could not be said of the creative arts. As if to compensate for their political lives, East German artists filled their canvases with colour. This is not to say that East German art was no more than a political statement (whether for or against the regime), because their work was every bit as interesting as that produced by their western counterparts, but it is true that they operated under very different conditions.

In the West, in contrast, artists were given free range, and made the most of this freedom. This is nowhere better illustrated than in the field of architecture. In virtually every city exciting modern buildings were constructed, often to mark important events, as in the case of the Munich Olympic Stadium (built for the 1972 Olympics), or to house important West German institutions, such as the Berlin **Philharmonie**, and the **Kongresshalle**, known by Berliners as the **schwangere Muschel** (pregnant mussel). At the same time, the city centres were rebuilt, creating wide roads, underground car parks and ring roads to accommodate the age of the car.

Problems of unification

The legacy of the East German regime gave the newly united Germany a number of headaches. Restoration was, and still is, the name of the game: Dresden's **Semmeroper** and the cathedral, for instance, have been undergoing intensive conservation and reconstruction programmes. Neglect has led to virtually all towns and cities in the East being swathed in green meshing as building work goes on underneath. Finally, the particular issues raised by Berlin have led to virtually the entire city becoming the biggest building site in Europe. Not only that, but the move from Bonn to Berlin has resulted in the **Reichstag** being rebuilt by the British architect Norman Foster. Meanwhile, the old **Potsdamer Platz**, in the heart of Berlin, which had been cleared to make way for the Wall in 1961, is now being intensively rebuilt.

Modern German artists

As always, it is difficult to predict which of the current batch of artists in Germany will go on to be remembered as 'greats' in the years to come. Likewise it is hard to talk of any specific movements or styles developing in the last decades of the 20th century. One area which has become quite important for contemporary German artists has been 'action art' or 'performance art' (known as 'happenings' in German), where a piece of work is displayed in public, with the reactions of passers-by being an integral part of the work. Joseph Beuys (1921–1986) set the ball rolling here, paddling across the Rhine in a dug-out canoe as an artistic statement. The Cologne artist H.A. Schult also provoked a great deal of interest with his *Fetisch Auto* action, where he erected a golden car, complete with angel wings, on top of a tower. Finally, Anselm Kiefer (born 1945) has made quite a name for himself with his *Bildkörper* (picture bodies), which are three dimensional pictures using a wide variety of materials, and his huge sculptures, such as *Zweistromland* (Mesopotamia), an eight-metre long bookcase weighing over 30 tons.

The avant garde scene is particularly strong in Germany, too, with many artists striving to attract attention towards their works through shock tactics, or new combinations of audio and visual presentation. Names such as Rebecca Horn (born 1945), Jörg Immendorf (born 1945) and Günter Uecker are all to be found in the media at regular intervals. Equally important here is the north

German village of Worpswede, which has been a centre of modern art since the 1920s and is the spiritual home for many of today's avant-gardists. Finally, look out for the 'documenta' if you are visiting Kassel. This is an international exhibition of contemporary art, held every five years, which is designed to showcase the best of the modern artists in Germany.

GLOSSARY

die Architektur *architecture*
das Schloss (Schlösser) *palace*
der Dom (-e) *cathedral*
die Kirche (-n) *church*
der Baustil (-e) *building style*
bauen *to build*
das Gebäude (-n) *building*
die Kunst *art*

der Künstler (-) / die Künstlerin (-nen) *artist*
das Gemälde (-n) *painting*
die Plastik (-s) *sculpture*
in Öl / Aquarell *in oils / watercolours*
die Bewegung (-en) *movement*
die Galerie (-n) *gallery*
das Museum (Museen) *museum*

Taking it further

There are, of course, countless guides to the art and architecture of Europe, but the most fun can be had from seeing great works and great buildings 'in the flesh'. One of the advantages of the federal system is that the art galleries and museums of virtually every German city of note can boast a fine collection of art and sculpture, and fine buildings can been seen in them also, despite the damage of the war.

For the best collections, however, the following galleries and museums are especially important. Some of them can be 'visited' online.

To see some of the early masters, such as Dürer or Cranach, you can do far worse than to visit the **Alte Pinakothek** in Munich (www.stmukwk.bayern.de/kunst/museen/pinalt.html), or perhaps the **Gemäldegalerie Alte Meister** in Dresden, both of which boast fine collections.

If the Romantic period interests you, then you have a great choice. The **Galerie der Romantik**, housed in Schloß Charlottenburg in Berlin (www.tarantula.smb.spk-berlin.de/gdr), is probably the best, with a huge collection of Caspar David Friedrich paintings, as well as good examples by Schinkel and the other notable Romantics. A close second, however, is the **Gemäldegalerie Neue Meister** in Dresden, which also has a large collection of Caspar David Friedrich paintings. Finally, the **Neue Pinakothek** in Munich houses many of Karl Spitzweg's best-loved works (www.stmukwk.bayern.de/kunst/museen/ pinneu.html), while the **Museum Georg Schäfer** in Schweinfurt is one of the largest private collections of art in Germany, with many important works by all of the great German artists of the 19th and early 20th centuries. It has a website at www.swin.de/kuku/mgs.

Bringing things into the 20th century, a good range of Expressionist art can be seen at the **Staatsgalerie moderner Kunst**, a wing of the **Haus der Kunst** in Munich. The **Kunstmuseum Bonn** concentrates on the group of artists now known as the **Rheinische Expressionisten**, notably Macke. Finally, as the only uniquely German architectural movement, it is fitting that Bauhaus should now have a museum devoted to its designs. The **bauhaus-archiv museum für gestaltung** is located in **Klingelhöferstraße** in Berlin, and has a suitably designed website at www.bauhaus-archiv.de.

5 | GERMAN MUSIC

In the world of music Germany enjoys a reputation that is second to none. The regions of Germany and Habsburg Austria between them produced many composers of talent and repute, and a handful of men who have come to be venerated as masters of their craft: few would claim not to have heard of names like Bach, Mozart and Beethoven, and the majority would be familiar with these composers' best-loved tunes, if only because so many have provided the soundtrack to the most successful films and TV advertisements. It is not at all uncommon for people nowadays, when they hear a piece of classical music, apparently for the first time, to exclaim: 'Oh yes, that's the music for *******!' (At this point insert the name of the currently in vogue brand of chocolate, beer or cars, and you'll know what I am talking about!)

Vorspiel: The contemporary scene

It would be fair to say that, whatever its musical pedigree, Germany is no longer considered a centre of music nowadays. For most people in Europe, at least, their only contact with contemporary German music is through the Eurovision Song Contest, or perhaps the freaks on '*Eurotrash*'. The appearance of Gildo Horn, the long-haired eccentric, singing '**Gildo hat euch lieb**' (loosely translated as 'Gildo loves ya') in the 1998 Eurovision Song Contest, will have done little to overturn the impression that German music is totally rubbish (in fact, public opinion in Germany was neatly divided, too, over the value of his appearance as Germany's representative that year!). Other Eurovision entrants in recent years to have achieved a degree of fame beyond German national boundaries include the soft rock band Münchner Freiheit (named after a **U-Bahn** stop in Munich) a few years ago, and the guitar-strumming teenager Nicole back in 1982, who won the contest that year. In terms of commercial success, Nena's hit '**99 Luftballons**' (99 Red Balloons) was a flash in the pan, with only the techno-bands such as Kraftwerk in the 1980s and Sash enjoying success in the 1990s.

In fact the contemporary music scene in Germany is far more varied than that. Admittedly bands singing in English have enjoyed the lion's share of chart success in the last 20–30 years, but Germany has a healthy supply of home-grown artists and groups. BAP, for instance, who sing in their Kölsch dialect (a German text is included in their albums for fans), have been very successful. Also popular in recent years has been the rock group Pur, which achieved particularly healthy sales with its post-unification hit '**Neue Brücken**' (new bridges). As soloists, Herbert Grönemeyer (who played the naive correspondent in the Second World War submarine film 'Das Boot'), and Udo Lindenberg have enjoyed great success in recent years, as has the **Liedermacher** (song maker) Wolf Biermann, who has been in conflict with both the East German and the West German authorities since he began his career singing politically motivated protest songs in the 1960s. Finally, a harder edge can be found in the music of heavy rock/heavy metal bands and artists such as Die toten Hosen (literally: dead trousers) and Nina Hagen, or the relatively new phenomenon of German-language rap: the all-girl group Tic-Tac-Toe hits '**Ich find' dich Scheiße**' and '**Verpiß dich**' (you probably don't need a dictionary to find out what the titles mean in English!) caused particular offence among members of the older generation, but were all the more successful among teenagers as a result. Also worthy of mention, perhaps, is the group die 3. Generation, not so much because of their hits (most successful to date was the song '**Vater, wo bist Du?**' ('Where are you, father?'), but because the group is made up of a German, a Turk and a Croat – a real indication of the multicultural aspect of modern German life.

But where has the contemporary scene come from? What is Germany's musical heritage precisely? The golden age of German music was, of course, the Classical era. Although an examination of these centuries could easily fill whole volumes (and often has), we will have to satisfy ourselves with a brief set of snapshots of the most important developments and personalities in German music.

Ouvertüre: 20th-century composers

It is worth beginning this tour with a brief examination of 'Modern Classical' music in Germany, because this neatly bridges the gap between the Baroque pomp of, say, Johann Sebastian Bach and the modern dance music of Sash. Two more or less contemporary composers are worthy of examination here.

Carl Orff (1895–1982)

Carl Orff is perhaps the only truly 20th-century composer in Germany to have achieved worldwide fame. He was born on 10 July 1895 in Munich and in 1913 attended the Munich **Akademie der Tonkunst** (literally 'Academy of Sound Art'). He quickly established a reputation as a competent musician and talented composer. He especially favoured choral work, and was fascinated by the medieval music of plainsong, both Latin and German. He was the conductor of the Munich Bach Society, and was inspired by this to develop an arrangement of the medieval Latin poem 'Carmina Burana', first performed in June 1937.

The strident chorus of 'O fortuna' which opens and closes the piece has been used in a number of films, most notably as the *leitmotif* (see 'Wagner' for an explanation of this term) accompanying the exploits of King Arthur in John Boorman's film 'Excalibur'.

Karlheinz Stockhausen (born 1929)

Stockhausen is the man who most successfully brought composition in Germany into the electronic age. As such, it is difficult to define him as a 'classical' composer, but his works are (usually) scored in a conventional manner, even if the music itself is often far from conventional. One particularly important Stockhausen project is an (as yet incomplete) opera cycle on the nature of life, called '**Licht – die sieben Tage der Woche**' (Light – the Seven Days of the Week).

It is also the right time to mention the vibrant classical scene in Germany today: despite the effect of the Nazi period on musical production – most composers and works were banned as degenerate; musicians and conductors of Jewish origin were killed or forced into exile; many concert halls and opera houses were destroyed – post-war Germany recovered from these setbacks. She is now home to a number of world-renowned orchestras, foremost being the Berliner Philharmoniker which enjoyed the leadership of the distinguished conductor Herbert von Karajan. But many major cities host **Land**-funded orchestras, while the main broadcasting corporations also offer patronage to highly talented ensembles. In terms of buildings, too, Germany boasts some of the finest concert theatres and opera houses in Europe, many of which had to be rebuilt after the war. The Hamburger Opernhaus is the oldest surviving, having been built in 1678, but the Frankfurter Alte Oper, the Münchener Nationaltheater or the radically modern Berliner Philharmonie, to name just a few, are musical centres of worldwide importance. Moreover, many of the conservatories and academies formed during the great Classical period of German musical creativity are still training young musicians of great talent.

Finally, it should not be forgotten that the German people in general are still a great musical folk. As well as being very keen concert-goers, they attend many annual musical events such as the **Donaueschinger Musiktage** (Donauesching Music Days).

Erster Satz: Back to the roots

Now our tour will take us back to the point where individuals began to make a living out of musical production for public entertainment. We begin, therefore, in the Middle Ages with the courtly poets.

Minnesang und Meistersang

In early medieval times the **Minnesänger** (see Chapter 3) produced a great range of lyrical poetry which would sometimes have been accompanied by simple tunes on the lute or wind instruments like recorders. Later on the **Meistersänger** tried to keep up the tradition handed to them from their knightly predecessors. The Master Singer Hans Sachs (1494–1576), who had been a cobbler in Nuremburg before beginning his musical training, is known to have produced hundreds of compositions but they, like the poetry he and his colleagues wrote, were very stilted and formal. Meanwhile, on the streets, **Bänkelsänger** (literally: bench singers) began to use **Volkslieder** (popular songs containing traditional and contemporary themes) as a form of political protest. They began a tradition of musical protest which is still a vibrant feature of German society even today.

Ecclesiastical music

Also there was the church. For many hundreds of years the only form of music to be found in churches in Germany, like elsewhere in medieval Europe, was the plainsong of the clergy and the monks or nuns in religious establishments. This was, naturally enough for the day, in Latin, and certainly was not intended to entertain the worshippers, but rather to glorify God. Slowly more expression came into these services, and as early as the 9th century organs were being installed in the cathedrals of Aachen and Straßburg (Strasbourg) to accompany the worshippers. But the pace of change was slow.

What changed all this was the Reformation. The Protestant church, founded on Luther's objections to Roman Catholicism, evolved into an altogether more 'people-friendly' place (although you might not consider three-hour services in cold churches particularly friendly) and it was in this environment that the first developments leading to Germany's great period of Classical music began.

Zweiter Satz: Baroque and the organ

The organ quickly established itself as the foremost instrument of German religious music: a school of German organ music was essentially created by Samuel Scheidt (1587–1654), of Halle, in Saxony, who devised a system for the notation of organ music which is still in use today; at the same time, Johann Schein (1586–1630) was being influenced by the music of the (already well-advanced) Italian Baroque, and imported the passion of the southern music into the more austere Lutheran tradition.

Later, Johann Froberger (1616–1667), Dietrich Buxtehude (1637–1707), Johann Pachelbel (1653–1706) and Georg Telemann (1681–1767) all produced increasingly sophisticated compositions, with Pachelbel's work being probably the best known today. These men, however, can all be viewed as forerunners of the greatest of Germany's organ composers, Johann Sebastian Bach.

Johann Sebastian Bach (1685–1750)

Bach was a great talent even as a child. Born in Eisenach in Thüringen, he was orphaned at the age of ten. He was twice married, and managed to produce a grand total of 22 children in his lifetime, much apart from any music he produced!

Bach produced many important organ pieces while engaged at the court of Weimar, the most famous of which is perhaps the Toccata und Fugue in D minor. Later, in 1717 he was promoted to Director of Music at the court of Cöthen, where he composed a number of orchestral pieces, including the six Brandenburg concertos and four orchestral suites, the third of which includes the piece of music known nowadays as Air on the G String. As Director of Music at the St Thomas music school in Leipzig (from 1723), he wrote literally hundreds of cantatas: short choral or organ pieces to be sung or played during the long Lutheran church services. Some famous cantatas, such as '**Herz und Mund und Tat und Leben**' (literally: 'Heart and Mouth and Deed and Life', but better known in English as 'Jesu, Joy of Man's Desiring') and '**Ein feste Burg ist unser Gott**' ('A safe Stronghold is our God') are still sung to much-loved English hymns. Finally, Bach's oratorios, the two passions – of St John (1723) and St Matthew – and his Christmas and Easter Oratorios (1734), have become hugely popular pieces with Bach choral societies all over Germany and the world.

Some 200 years later, Richard Wagner was to write of Bach and his influence on the spiritual life of Germany:

> Will man die wunderbare Eigentümlichkeit, Kraft und Bedeutung des deutschen Geistes in einem unvergleichlich

beredten Bilde erfassen, so blicke man scharf und sinnvoll auf die ... Erscheinung des musikalischen Wundermannes Sebastian [sic] Bach.

(If one wants to sum up the wonderful originality, vitality and significance of the German spirit in one incomparably eloquent image, then one should look keenly and meaningfully at the appearance of the musical marvel Sebastian Bach.)

Dritter Satz: The symphony

In the 1700s, music production was divided between the Protestant north and east, with its long Lutheran services, and the Catholic south and west, where the music reflected the opulence of the Roman mass. The centre of this second group was the capital of the Habsburg dynasty, Vienna. Although the music of Austria is technically outside this guide to German culture, it is virtually impossible to discuss German music without referring to the influence of the Viennese composers, and of Vienna as the capital of 18th century-musical life. Not only did they have a profound effect on their (truly) German counterparts, but they pushed back the boundaries of world music as a whole. Josef Haydn (1732–1809), especially, was the impulse behind the 'First Viennese School'. After many years of service under the patronage of the Austro-Hungarian von Esterhazy family, and a number of visits to London, Haydn set himself up in Vienna. He is remembered especially as the man who took the symphony to its most technically brilliant conclusion: he wrote over 100 of them. The 104th, the London Symphony was written during one of his stays in Britain, during which time he was awarded an honorary doctorate in music at Oxford University. He was greatly admired by Mozart, and won even greater praise for his oratorios (sometimes known as symphony-cantatas, because of their religious content) '**Die Schöpfung**' ('The Creation', 1798) and '**Die Jahreszeiten**' ('The Seasons', 1801).

Josef Haydn – Das Deutschlandlied

Haydn set to music a popular nationalistic poem by August Heinrich Hoffmann which begins with the now infamous words **'Deutschland, Deutschland über alles'**. Like many things which have been tarnished by later association with Hitler and his Nazi party, the **Deutschlandlied** as it came to be known was no more than a song urging the separate German states to forget about their differences and come together (hence, Germany above all else). The tune is well known to us as 'Austria' and is sung to the popular hymn 'Glorious Things of Thee are Spoken' in English-speaking churches. Later, from 1918 until 1946, the same tune was also used to accompany the Austrian national anthem the first line of which was then **'Gott erhalte Franz den Kaiser'** ('God preserve Franz the Emperor'). After the Second World War Germany retained the *Deutschlandlied* as her national anthem, but dropped the contentious first verse.

"The German Nationalhymne, text by August Heinrich Hoffmann von Fallersleben, melody by Josef Haydn." The opening line reads ' Unity and Justice and Freedom for the German Fatherland."

Ludwig van Beethoven (1770–1827)

It was the genius Mozart who recognized the talent of the young Beethoven. When he first heard the boy improvising on a musical theme during a visit to Vienna, he is said to have advised members of the audience: 'Keep your eyes on him; some day he will give the world something to think about.' Beethoven had been sent to Vienna to study under Haydn, in the autumn of 1792, and although their relationship was, by all accounts, less than fruitful, each acknowledged his respect for the other's work. Haydn reported in a letter dated 23 November 1793: 'On the basis of these pieces [sheets of music had been sent with the letter], expert and amateur alike cannot but admit that Beethoven will in time become one of the greatest musical artists in Europe.' During this first period in Vienna Beethoven produced many famous piano sonatas (including the 'Moonlight' and the 'Pathétique' sonatas), his first piano concertos, and works for string quartets, and the first two of his nine symphonies. But these achievements were marred by the onset of the deafness which threatened to end his career.

After this crisis he produced his third symphony, and his only opera score ('**Fidelio, oder die eheliche Liebe**' – 'Fidelio, or marital love', 1805). The symphony, in E flat major, was to be dedicated to Napoleon Bonaparte, whom Beethoven admired greatly: greatly, that is, until Napoleon proclaimed himself Emperor of the French Republic in 1804. Upon hearing this news, Beethoven ripped up the title page of the symphony and renamed it the '**Sinfonia eroica**', as it is still known.

Despite failing health and eventual deafness, Beethoven's creativity remained undiminished. This is perhaps the key to his continued popularity: one phrase of his Fifth Symphony was used by the BBC throughout the Second World War to symbolise victory (imagine 'da-da-da **dah**', the Morse code for V), and the Sixth Symphony, known as the 'Pastoral', reflects his love of the natural world. In the autumn of 1813 Wellington's victory over French troops in the Peninsula war prompted the symphony entitled '**Wellingtons Sieg oder die Schlacht bey Vittoria**' ('Wellington's Victory or the Battle of Vitoria'). Then, some 10 years later Beethoven produced the work which many see as the crowning achievement of his life, the Ninth Symphony (see box), which is credited with ushering in a new period in European music.

German symphonic composition: Beethoven's Ninth Symphony

This symphony, in D minor (Op. 125) is referred to as the 'Choral Symphony', with a stirring final choral movement based on Schiller's poem **Ode an die Freiheit** (*Ode to Freedom*). The title was changed to **Ode an die Freude** (*Ode to Joy*) in Beethoven's version, to avoid any political repercussions from the authorities who were increasingly worried by the prospect of revolution in Germany. For many people it is the quintessential piece of German music.

Moreover, it is this music which has been proposed as a possible 'national' anthem for a united Europe, which is testament to Beethoven's popularity and ability, even if you do not approve of the political sentiment!

Vierter Satz: The German opera

Germany has been a very fruitful ground for opera. As early as the 1600s, Heinrich Schütz (1585–1672) – a contemporary of the organists Scheidt and Schein – produced the first German opera. Unfortunately the score of this work, **'Dafne'** (1627), has been lost. Although others produced operas worthy of note in a more detailed study, we will jump forward some 200 years, to examine one of the most fascinating musical figures of all.

Wolfgang Amadeus Mozart (1756–1791)

Born on 27 January 1756 in Salzburg, but to a Bavarian family, Mozart was christened Johannes Chrysostomus Wolfgangus Theophilus. It was soon clear to all observers that the young boy was an amazing musical prodigy. But his precocious talent seems to have attracted almost as much censure as praise, and Mozart struggled most of his life to make a living through his music. Despite the fact that he died at the young age of 35, he produced some 600 works, sometimes composing whole symphonies in his head which he simply wrote down when he got the chance.

Mozart's operas astonished the world of opera when they were first performed and still enchant audiences today. Many of the *libretti* (the texts upon which the operas are based) were in fact in Italian, which was considered *the* operatic language at the time, and many experts swear that the German language operas sound different to those originally conceived in Italian. The first of the greats, 'Idomeneo', was premiered in 1781. After the premiere of **'Die Entführung aus dem Serail'** ('Abduction from the Harem') in 1782, the next four operas – **'Le Nozze di Figaro'** ('The Marriage of Figaro', 1786), **'Don Giovanni'** (1787), **'Cosi fan Tutte'** ('Thus do All Women', 1790) and **'Die Zauberflöte'** ('The Magic Flute', 1791) were all products of Mozart's most proficient final years, as he wrote feverishly in failing health. Mozart's operas revolutionised the world of music with radical use of key – he was the first to link the key of A minor with scenes of sensuality and seduction, for instance – and a fine appreciation of the dramatic potential of the opera.

But Mozart was prolific in every area of music, rarely bound by any one convention or another. He created pieces of great solemnity or, as in the case of the famous Serenade No. 13, '**Eine kleine Nachtmusik**' ('A Little Serenade'), of exquisite lightness. In many ways, Mozart was a man possessed, who was convinced (with some justification) that his rivals were out to get him: the theory was fancifully proposed in the successful film 'Amadeus' in the 1980s. Whatever the truth, with the death of Mozart in Vienna on 5 December 1791, the musical world prematurely lost one of its finest talents.

The Romantics

Sitting neatly between the Classical genius of Mozart and the modernist tendencies of Richard Wagner (see following section) the operas of the German Romantics provided an important steppingstone, and influenced Wagner more than he might have cared to admit. Like their counterparts in art and literature, the Romantics looked to their experiences of the world around them to inspire their creativity. They often composed musical accompaniments to poetic work, paintings or novels and might themselves have been talented poets or artists. Although the Romantic movement affected all areas of German music – Beethoven's later work, for instance, is considered 'Romantic' – it is the opera which was most radically influenced by this phenomenon. Carl Maria von Weber (1786–1826) and Heinrich Marschner (1795–1861), for instance, produced operas which continued Mozart's liberalising process and set the tone for Wagner's mythical flights of fancy in later years. Von Weber's '**Der Freischütz**' ('The Free Shooter'), which premiered in the **Berliner Schauspielhaus** on 18 June 1821, is a tale of nationalist fervour, and contained folk songs, catchy melodies and marvellous supernatural scenes in the Wolf's Glen. Von Weber died in London on 5 June 1826 and was buried in Dresden, where a young Richard Wagner gave a graveside address.

Richard Wagner (1813–1883)

Although Wagner was born only two decades after the death of Mozart, most people (mistakenly) regard him as a modern, even 20th century, composer. Born in Leipzig on 22 May 1813, Wagner saw a performance of Beethoven's '**Fidelio**' while still a youth and was inspired by the artistic energy of the opera.

But even in his youth Wagner was hot-headed and lived a lavish lifestyle: he was frequently forced to flee bad debts, irate husbands (of his numerous lovers), and even the authorities (following the revolution of 1848). This last trouble took him to exile in Switzerland for 10 years, during which time he composed most of his great works. He also wrote about the opera, and developed the theory of the **Gesamtkunstwerk** (whole work of art). To Wagner it was not enough merely to write the score to someone else's *libretto* (the story), then allow another person to choreograph the action, and yet another to design the set, etc. etc. He had to have a hand in every stage of the creative process, and was meticulous in the level of detail he included in every one of his **Kunstdramen** (music dramas), as he liked to call his works.

After only modest success with his first, rather traditional operas, Wagner despaired of making it big. But driven by an unshakeable belief in his own vision of opera – many called it arrogance – he persisted. Real acknowledgement of his talent followed the premiere of '**Der fliegende Holländer**' ('The Flying Dutchman') in Dresden on 2 January 1843, which secured Wagner his first proper musical post, as **Kapellmeister** (court musician) at the court in Dresden.

By the 1850s Wagner was in exile in Switzerland. He began work on a monumental project based around the medieval epic tale, the **Nibelungenlied** (see Chapter 3). He not only wanted these operas to be true to his **Gesamtkunstwerk** principle, but he also conceived the works to be played together over the course of a four-day festival. The fact that he would have to build a theatre capable of accommodating the operas seems not to have daunted Wagner, so sure was he of his own talents! Such a huge project could not be created overnight: in the meantime he published

Wagner's epic cycle *Der Ring des Nibelungen*

With the full Ring-cycle of the Nibelungen, German opera reached a peak of spectacle which still takes the breath away today – if you can sit through four days of opera, that is! The first evening of a full Wagner festival brings the **Vorspiel**, '**Das Rheingold**', which tells of the fashioning of the all-powerful ring while the gods, Wotan, Fricka, Freia and others, wrangle over the fate of the humans involved, and the cursed ring.

'**Die Walküre**' then depicts Siegmund's gaining of Wotan's sword and the beautiful Sieglinde, and his eventual death. This part of the cycle includes the famous 'Ride of the Valkyries'.

Part III '**Siegfried**', follows the fate of Siegfried, the orphaned son of Siegmund and Sieglinde. He has been brought up by the dwarf Mime, whose brother Alberich first stole the gold to create the ring. Siegfried kills the dragon Fafner, and learns of Mime's evil plans. Later, he awakens Brünnhilde, who has been in a deep sleep, with a kiss.

Finally, '**Götterdämmerung**' ('Twilight of the Gods') tells of the fate of the ring, and the various bloody plots to possess its power. Even Brünnhilde betrays her lover Siegfried, who is murdered by Hagen; but he too dies as Brünnhilde returns the ring to the depths of the Rhine and ushers in the end of the gods' time on earth.

Confused? Don't worry, if you ever get the chance to see the cycle you will have some 18 hours of action, accompanied by some of the most stirring music ever scored for opera, to get to grips with the complicated plot. Sit back, and enjoy!

'**Tristan und Isolde**' in 1859 (inspired by yet another affair, the score is considered by many to be the most sensuous music ever written in the West) and '**Die Meistersinger von Nürnberg**' ('The Master Singers of Nuremberg') in 1867. It was largely thanks to the patronage of the Bavarian King Ludwig II that Wagner was ever able to build his **Festspielhaus** at Bayreuth, in Bavaria, and conduct the first full cycle of the '**Ring des Nibelungen**' between

13 and 17 August 1876 (see separate box for more details). After his final opera, '**Parsifal**', which was performed in 1882, Wagner's place in the pantheon of world music was assured. Many contemporary audiences described a performance of a Wagnerian opera, quite simply, as intoxicating. It is unfortunate for him, of course, that his anti-Semitism and later following by Hitler and the Nazis has often overshadowed his achievements, because Wagner – for all his faults – was a true genius of opera and has made as great a mark on that particular form of musical composition as any other German.

Fünfter Satz: The *Singspiel* and the *Lied*

Beethoven's later compositions were already beginning to outgrow the period known as Classical music when the Romantic wave swept across Europe in general, and, in its German guise as **Sturm und Drang**, across Germany in particular. For centuries the simple folksong had been very popular in Germany, both as entertainment (the **Singspiel** (song play) had been an early form of opera there) and protest. In due course, the **Lied** (song) became an important musical feature of the Romantic movement. It became fashionable to draw from folk-tales and poetry when composing, and the period also saw a huge revival in the work of some of the old masters just mentioned: Bach's complete works were published for the first time in the early 1800s, for instance, and his music enjoyed renewed popularity. The man behind this particular revival was Felix Mendelssohn.

Felix Mendelssohn (1809–1847)

Mendelssohn was born on 3 February 1809 in Hamburg to a well-off family. As is the case with many of the masters mentioned here, his talent was recognised early, when his **Overture to 'Midsummer Night's Dream'** was published in 1825. He also gained recognition for his Scherzo, and the whole world knows his '**Wedding March**', even if only the first few bars! As a student at the University of Berlin he studied under the great philosopher Hegel, developed a strong friendship with Heinrich Heine and even met the famous Goethe himself. On 11 March 1829 he conducted his own arrangement of Bach's St Matthew Passion at the **Berliner Singakademie** (Berlin Academy of Song), the first time it had been performed since Bach's days. In the same year he travelled to Scotland, where he met Sir Walter Scott, and was inspired to write a **'Hebrides overture'** (premiere 1832), although his **'Italian' Symphony (No. 4)** is an altogether sunnier piece of music, as befits the subject-matter. Mendelssohn then deepened his links with Britain with the 1842 **'Scottish' Symphony**, which he dedicated to Queen Victoria. Indeed, the first public performance of his great **'Elijah'** oratorio took place in Birmingham, on 26 August 1846. Just a few months later, on 4 November 1847, he died in Leipzig. The Conservatory (musical academy) which he founded in 1843 ensured that he left a vital legacy to German music which continues today.

Robert Schumann (1810–1856)

Schumann is another of the key figures of German Romantic music. As well as being a gifted musician in his own right, he was responsible for establishing the principle of music criticism in Germany when, in 1834, he began to edit the journal *Neue Zeitschrift für Musik*. With Mendelssohn he helped to rediscover older works (including a lost symphony by Schubert) and was the first to recognise the talent of the young Brahms. Tragically, he went insane and on 27 February 1854, tormented by voices, threw himself into the Rhine at Düsseldorf. He survived this incident, but lived out his life in a mental asylum.

More than any other German, Schumann composed a great many popular **Lieder** (although it should be noted that Franz Schubert established the **Lied** as a musical form, but, being Austrian, we will set him aside from this study). He was married to Clara, an accomplished concert pianist in her own right, and had enjoyed a promising career as a pianist himself, before an injury to his hand forced him to concentrate on composition. He had a fine sense of how to make his songs easy on the ear, and was quick to learn, which virtually guaranteed him success at a time when the Romantic **Lied** was in great demand. His 1840 **'Liederkreis'** (Song Cycle, Op. 39) was based on a set of poems by Josef Eichendorff, and another cycle known as **'Dichterliebe'** was equally popular. In addition to these works, his Piano Concerto is still popular, and pieces from the work '**Kinderszenen**' (Children's Scenes) are popular among students of the piano. After Schumann's death, Clara inspired Brahms to continue his own career, when he composed some of his best work.

Johannes Brahms (1833–1897)

Born in Hamburg on 7 May 1833, Brahms grew up in humble surroundings but became one of the most acclaimed composers of his generation. As has been mentioned already, he became a close friend of the Schumanns, who first broadcast his talent in the 1850s. His first major work, the '**Deutsches Requiem**' ('German Requiem', 1868) for his dead mother, was quickly followed by works which established his reputation: the 1871 '**Triumphlied**' ('Song of Triumph'), celebrating the victory of the Franco-Prussian war, and his first Symphony, in C minor. Many say that Brahms carried on in the tradition of Beethoven, and called this symphony Beethoven's Tenth. The repeated theme of the last movement is especially well known, and was adopted by the British Labour Party as the theme for their 1992 election campaign. It didn't help them, however – they lost! Brahms wrote three other symphonies, two piano concertos and a double concerto for violin and cello. In his later years, his work became increasingly personal and almost introverted, inspired by his close friendship with the now-widowed Clara Schumann. In the 1890s he produced a fine Clarinet Quintet and a Trio for the same instrument, as well as several **Lieder** and Intermezzos for piano. When Clara Schumann died in 1896, he seemed unable to get over her loss and died himself on 3 April 1897.

Brahms was often dismissed as an anti-Romantic, but only because he rather disapproved of the direction orchestral music was taking at the time, preferring a heavier, more 'Classical' style. In fact, his music was deeply personal, always inspired by his friendships, his loves (he never married, despite several relationships) and, later, the loss of friends and family. In this sense, Brahms was more of a Romantic composer than many of his detractors. Although his work can seem rather heavy, compared to his contemporaries, perseverance is to be recommended.

Finale

So rich is the contribution that Germany has made to the world of music that we have, by necessity, excluded many composers of note, including the German-speaking Austrians: the operas of Giacomo Meyerbeer, E.T.A. Hoffmann, Richard Strauss or Anton Bruckner, the waltzes of the Johann Strausses, Liszt's **Lieder**, Gustav Mahler, George Handel, Arnold Schönberg, Franz Lehár, Hugo Wolf … the list goes on and on. What this chapter has tried to demonstrate is that the subject of German music, especially when looking at her classical composers, is a fascinating area of research which will repay further reading … and listening!

GLOSSARY

die Musik *music*
klassische Musik *classical music*
der Komponist (-en) *composer*
das Konzert (-e) *concert*
ein Instrument spielen *to play an instrument*

das Orchester (-) *orchestra*
ein Stück (-e) Musik *a piece of music*
die Oper (-n) *opera*
Musik zuhören *to listen to music*
der Schlager (-) *hit*
der Rocksänger (-) *rock singer*

Taking it further

There are countless books and CDs with which to deepen your interest in German music, of course. Any encyclopedia, such as the *Oxford Companion to Music*, will contain useful biographies and catalogues of a composer's work.

John Suchet's fictional biography of Beethoven has been praised as an interesting and useful background to the period of Germany's greatest musical creativity. It is called *The Last Master* and is published by Warner Books in the UK, ISBN 0-7515-1980-4.

For Mozart fans, Edward J. Dent's *Mozart's Operas* is still considered one of the standard reference works, even though the first edition was published in 1913.

6 TRADITIONS, FESTIVALS AND FOLKLORE

Like all European countries, Germany has a rich tradition of celebrations and festivals, with a whole range of events throughout the year celebrated at both local and national level. As we shall see, many of these are Christian ceremonies which are shared with other cultures in the western world, but they also have aspects that are unique to them. Others celebrate great historical or political events that happened within Germany, while a number are simply traditions which date back to beyond living memory! As well as these common, very public festivals and holidays, we will also look at the various rites of passage celebrated in the more intimate environment of the German family.

Alongside these, the Germans have long been interested in their home-grown fairy tales and nursery rhymes. The Grimm brothers, Hans and Jakob, began the process of recording as many folktales as they could trace in the 19th century, with many of these stories eventually travelling beyond Germany's borders: most readers will be familiar with versions of the story known in Germany as *Hänsel und Gretel*, for instance, or that of *Rotkäppchen* (*Little Red Riding Hood*), thanks to the work of the brothers.

Finally, we need, as always, to bear in mind the rather fragmented nature of Germany's past to recognise that there is a large number of regional differences in the way Germans celebrate all these events. Even today, for instance, **Feiertage** (public holidays) are often different in the Catholic **Länder** in the south and west to those observed in the predominantly Protestant north and east. Wherever you go in Germany, however, you can be sure that a public holiday or a large celebration is not far away: to the visitor it can seem that the Germans live for their public holidays and, for all their reputation as a rather staid race, they love to party!

Von der Wiege bis zur Bahre: From the cradle to the grave

Birth

Like any culture, the Germans love to celebrate the birth of a child, but in recent years there have been growing worries that the birthrate has been in sharp decline. '**Die Deutschen sterben aus!**' ('the Germans are dying out') screamed the headlines just a few years ago, accompanied by gloomy predictions that, within 20 years, the population of Germany would be in terminal decline. Whether this was an accurate picture or not, the fact remains that fewer people are having babies nowadays in Germany, and large families – even in the Catholic regions – are becoming increasingly rare.

Confirmation

Despite a reduction in the influence of the churches in Germany, for many families a child's act of taking his or her place in the local congregation is still of great significance. In the Catholic regions, in particular, the occasion of the **erste Kommunion** (first communion) is accompanied by a large party at which the communicant receives gifts and money: some have even suggested that this is the principal motivation for many children nowadays!

First day at school

For many children in Germany, as with children around the world, the first day at school can be rather daunting. To soften the blow, they receive an **Einschulungstüte** (first-day-of-school bag), which is a brightly decorated cone of paper or card, often nearly as large as the child, which will contain shiny new pens, rulers, pencil sharpeners etc., but also sweets and perhaps a little money. In older photos of children receiving their **Tüte** in the 1920s and 1930s, they often stood next to a blackboard with the momentous date chalked on it, as a permanent record of the day. German schoolchildren at **Grundschule** (primary school) still carry quite distinctive **Schulranzen** (satchels) on their backs, and will often be given their satchel on this first day of school. (For more information on education in Germany see Chapter 9.)

The all-important driving licence

Getting a driving licence, an important symbol of growing independence, can be a lengthy and expensive business. In Germany young people are allowed to learn to drive a car after their 17th birthday. Before they may sit behind the wheel of a car, however, they are required to pass a theory test, which usually involves several weeks of classes. Even then, they are obliged to take driving lessons at a **Fahrschule** (driving school), where they will receive a mixture of theoretical and practical instruction. Finally, often as much as a year after they began the process, they will be required to undergo a rigorous driving test before they are allowed out on the roads on their own.

Marriage

For many people the next major landmark in their lives is when they decide that they want to get married. After the **Heiratsantrag** (proposal of marriage) has been made, usually by the young man, and a date has been set for the wedding, it is the **Polterabend** (literally: smashing evening) which begins the celebrations. This takes place on the night before the wedding, when the bride and groom invite their friends and family to a party during which the guests are encouraged to smash a load of crockery – don't worry, it is not normally the best china, but instead a specially produced inferior set! This practice is supposed to scare away any bad luck and thus give the couple a good start to their married life.

The next day the bride and groom make their way to the **Standesamt**, the civil registry office in the centre of town, where

the legal ceremony takes place. This ceremony is required by law, but many couples traditionally choose to go straight to their local church for a Christian blessing as well. This practice is a little less popular now than it was, but is not restricted to regular church-goers, by any means.

After another evening of partying, the couple leave to go on their **Flitterwoche** (honeymoon, but translating literally as 'sparkling week', referring to the fact that the marriage is new and presumably shiny).

Rund ums Jahr: All the year round

So what are the main German festivals and public holidays? Let's flick through the German calendar to see who is celebrating what, and when they're doing it. The dates which are public holidays for the whole country are indicated by an asterisk (*).

Januar

*1. Januar:
Silvester

Januar						
①	2	3	4	5	⑥	7
8	9	10	11	12	13	14
15	16	17	18	19	20	21
22	23	24	25	26	27	28
29	30	31				

Silvester is the German New Year celebrations, which actually begin on the night of 31 December, known as **Silvesterabend**. Two aspects of this celebration are of special note: one is a TV film, called 'Dinner for One'. Not only is the title of the film English, but all the dialogue is in English too – it is a simple story of a lonely widow who celebrates New Year with her imaginary, now-dead friends and her increasingly-drunk butler (he has to drink all the toasts for the imaginary guests). 'Dinner for One' is shown on virtually every television channel during the course of the evening, even twice on some stations, and is virtually compulsory viewing nowadays. More astonishing is the fact that most Germans cannot believe that the film is unknown outside Germany!

Silvester is also the biggest night for fireworks in Germany. In the same way that plates are smashed at the **Polterabend**, fireworks are supposed to frighten away any bad spirits at the beginning of the New Year. In recent years, however, people have voiced concerns over the amount of money which is wasted in the few short minutes after midnight.

One particularly nice greeting at this time of the year, whether on a card sent through the post, or when you talk to people early in the New Year, is to wish them **'einen guten Rutsch ins Neujahr'**, which means 'a good slide into the New Year', reflecting the fact that Germany typically enjoys snow and ice throughout the Christmas and New Year period!

6. Januar: Heilige Drei Könige

This is Epiphany, the day when the Three Kings are said to have visited the baby Jesus. For German families who have crib scenes over Christmas, therefore, this is the day that the models of the Kings and their entourage should reach the stable, having wandered all over the house during the Christmas festivities. Another interesting tradition on this day is that children dress up as the Three Kings and walk around their neighbourhood chalking the initials **K + M + B** (for Kaspar, Melchior and Balthasar) on doors, plus the year.

Februar

Karneval or Fasching

Februar						
			1	2	3	4
5	6	7	8	9	10	⑪
12	13	14	15	16	17	18
19	20	21	22	23	24	25
26	27	28				

Although it is known by different names around Germany, February sees the beginning of the carnival period. In places like Cologne,

Mainz and Munich, processions wend their way around the streets, with both participants and observers decked out in weird and wonderful costumes, and a merry time is had by all. So popular is the period of **Karneval** that the committees which run these events are covered by local and national TV stations in the run-up to the festivities. For a first-time visitor to Germany it can be quite a shock to turn up in the middle of **Karneval**, and woe betide any man who is wearing a tie ... in some areas he is likely to have it cut off by a young woman if he is not careful!

The origins of **Karneval** are not clear, but probably go back to pagan times in Germany. In Christian times it refers to the period before Lent, when the pious would fast up to Easter (the name is thought to come from the Latin for 'without meat'). In some areas the period is known as **Fasching**, or **Fastnacht**, but wherever you watch this revelling you can be sure that it is one time of the year, at least, where the Germans disprove the myth that they do not know how to enjoy themselves.

Officially the carnival period begins in November, at the 11th minute, of the 11th hour, of the 11th day, of the 11th month, to be precise! The run-up to the final days in February can be anticipated by many for weeks, with more and more **Gaudi** (the Bavarian term for the harmless tricks and games associated with **Fasching**) going on as time goes by. On the Thursday before **Aschermittwoch** (Ash Wednesday), for instance, the Lord Mayor of Cologne solemnly hands over the keys of the city to the carnival prince. From this moment on during the **drei Tollen Tage** (three mad days) anything can happen – groups of brightly coloured soldiers disobey every order they receive, strange decrees are issued, and partying is increasingly the order of the day. This climaxes a few days before Lent with the **Rosenmontag** parade, much revelling and drinking of alcohol, and not a little kissing of total strangers. You have been warned: if you are not one for public tomfoolery, then stay away from Germany during **Karneval**! At least wait until **Fastnachts-dienstag** (Shrove Tuesday), when the carnival prince hands the keys back to the Lord Mayor, and Germany returns to relative normality – until the following November.

März/April

März						
			1	2	3	4
5	6	7	8	9	10	11
12	13	14	15	16	17	18
19	20	21	22	23	24	25
26	27	28	29	30	31	

April						
						1
2	3	4	5	6	7	8
9	10	11	12	13	14	15
16	17	18	19	20	21	22
23	24	25	26	27	28	29
30						

*Karfreitag

This is the German Good Friday, the day on which Christ was crucified, and is the beginning of **Ostern**, the Easter weekend. It is still strictly observed by both major confessions, and is always a public holiday throughout Germany. The name comes from an old German word meaning 'worry' or 'mourning', and is linked to the modern English word 'care'.

*Ostersonntag

Easter is celebrated in Germany in much the same way as other Christian countries, with chocolate eggs and cute toy chicks vying for attention alongside the Christian message. German children especially look forward to the visit of the **Osterhase** (Easter hare), who brings the eggs. They will paint hard-boiled eggs, and decorate branches with small wooden eggs, in the run-up to Easter. Easter Monday is a public holiday too.

Mai

Mai						
	①	2	3	4	5	6
7	8	9	10	11	12	13
14	15	16	17	18	19	20
21	22	23	24	25	26	27
28	29	30				

*1. Mai:
Maitag

In common with many other European countries 1 May is the traditional labourers' holiday.

*Christi Himmelfahrt

Christ's Ascension, 40 days after Easter. This is a public holiday in all states.

Pfingsten

Another moveable feast, Whit Monday is a public holiday in most **Länder**.

Fronleichnam

This is the Feast of Corpus Christi, on the second Thursday after **Pfingsten**, and is observed in the Catholic states.

August

15. August:
Maria Himmelfahrt

August				
	1	2	3	4	5
6	7	8	9	10	11	12
13	14	⑮	16	17	18	19
20	21	22	23	24	25	26
27	28	29	30	31

The day of Mary's Assumption into heaven, observed in most
Catholic states.

Oktober

*3. Oktober:
Tag der
deutschen Einheit

Oktober						
1	2	③	4	5	6	7
8	9	10	11	12	13	14
15	16	17	18	19	20	21
22	23	24	25	26	27	28
29	30	31

This is Germany's newest holiday, introduced in 1991 following
unification the year before, and celebrates the Day of German
Unity. It replaced the holiday of the same name on 17 June, which
commemorated an uprising by citizens of East Germany in 1953.
Once Germany was reunited it was deemed unnecessary to mark
that particular day any longer, and the date of unification was an
obvious choice for the new holiday.

November

*1. November:
Allerheiligen

November				
			①	2	3	4
5	6	7	8	9	10	11
12	13	14	15	16	17	18
19	20	21	22	23	24	25
26	27	28	29	30

All Saints' Day, a public holiday throughout Germany.

Buß- und Bettag

This is the Day of Repentance and Prayer, on the third Wednesday
in November. It used to be observed throughout Germany, until it
was abolished in 1994 in all regions except Saxony.

Dezember

6. Dezember:
Nikolaustag

Dezember				
			1	2	3	4
5	⑥	7	8	9	10	11
12	13	14	15	16	17	18
19	20	21	22	23	㉔	㉕
26	27	28	29	30	31

For Germans, this is the beginning of the Christmas season. It is the
day when St. Nicholas brings his presents to the children, and it is
traditional to give a small gift on this day. Of course, by this time

Advent has begun, and German families will have been opening the windows of their Advent Calendars for six days already, and will be beginning to think about bringing a tree into the house for Christmas.

Weihnachten

As in many countries, the exact way of celebrating Christmas can vary from region to region and even from family to family. Certain elements are common to most families' celebrations, however. The **Christkindlmarkt** (Christ Child Market) or **Weihnachtsmarkt** (Christmas Market) is a popular place to buy hand-made decorations and presents, and to drink **Glühwein** (a potent mulled wine which translates as 'glowing wine' and is guaranteed to keep out the cold!). Even the smallest village may have its own **Markt**, but the biggest, and most famous, can be found in Cologne, Nuremburg and Munich. At these markets you may well hear **Weihnachtslieder** (Christmas carols), the most famous of which is 'Stille Nacht', known in English as 'Silent Night', which was written in 1818.

1. Stil - le Nacht, hei - li - ge Nacht! Al - les schläft, ein - sam wacht

nur das trau-te, hoch- hei - li - ge Paar, hol-der Kna-be im lok-ki-gen Haar,

schlaf in himm-li - scher Ruh,___ schlaf___ in himm-li-scher Ruh!

The story of '**Stille Nacht**' tells that the organ of the parish church of Oberndorf (technically just inside Austria, but in this instance nobody's quibbling) was broken, and on Christmas Eve of all days. The priest, Franz Gruber, was faced with the awful prospect of Christmas Mass without music; but his young trainee priest, Joseph Mohr, composed the world-famous words, and Gruber set them to music for two voices, choir and guitar. Within just a few years the simple carol had become loved throughout the world.

24. Dezember: Heiliger Abend

The 'hallowed eve' is the night when the **Christkind** (Christ child) will come. As everywhere else in the world, it is a night of great excitement and anticipation! In Germany this is supposed to be when the family put up their **Weihnachtsbaum** (Christmas tree), which must be a good **Tannenbaum** (fir).

*25. Dezember: Frohe Weihnachten!

The German word for Christmas comes from the medieval *wihen nachten*, or holy nights. Attendance at a church service is still a common part of many families' celebrations of Christmas, but the 25th is also the last day of the Christmas season (the day we know as Boxing Day is simply the **2. Weihnachstag** in Germany), leaving an extra day of relaxation before the build-up to **Silvester** on 31 December.

Some regional titbits

Finally, here are a few events worth looking out for if you happen to be in a particular part of Germany at the right time.

Januar

Villinger Fasnet

A parade of colourful and often quite scary costumes in the town of Villingen-Schwennigen in Baden Württemberg.

Aachener Karlsfest

Celebration of Charlemagne held in Aachen.

März

Schäfertanz

The Dance of the Shepherds in the picturesque town of Rothenburg ob der Tauber, with its medieval walls.

Thüringer Bachtage

A celebration of Bach's music in and around Weimar.

April

Baumblüte

One of many springtime festivals in Germany, this one takes place in Werder in Potsdam.

Mai

Meistertrunk

The Master Draught is a play portraying a true story from the 17th century when the town of Rothenburg ob der Tauber was saved from destruction.

Holzhauer- und Fuhrmannsfest

Festival of the Woodcutters and Ferrymen at Finsterbergen, near Eisenach in the Thüringer Wald.

Rattenfänger-Spiele

An open-air play recounting the famous story of the Pied Piper of Hameln (Hamelin).

Passionsspiel

The Oberammergau Passion Play is the most famous of many in Germany which enjoy a rich and long tradition. It is performed only every 10 years, with the next performance scheduled for 2010.

Juni

Kultursommer

Concerts and theatre performances in Oldenburg, near Bremen.

Parkfestspiele Sanssouci

Festival held in the grounds of Kaiser Wilhelm's great palace in Potsdam.

Händel-Festspiele

Concerts in Göttingen, Niedersachsen, to celebrate the works of this composer.

Kieler Woche

Week-long, world-famous regatta in Kiel, Schleswig-Holstein.

Juli

Wochenende an der Jade

A festival of music and watersports in Cuxhaven, far in the north.

Wagner-Festspiele

Daily performances of Wagner's works in his own festival hall in Bayreuth, Bavaria.

Ritterspiele

Medieval pageantry in Kiefersfelden, right on the Austrian border in Bavaria.

Friedensfest

Annual celebration of the end of the Thirty Years' War, held in Augsburg.

Berlinale

Germany's premiere film festival, at which the prestigious **Goldener Bär** (Golden Bear) awards are made.

Love Parade

One of Europe's biggest open air events, this is a pulsating procession of hundreds of thousands of young people, partying to techno music through the Brandenburg Gate.

August

Mainfest

Celebration of wines and other produce in and around Frankfurt.

Festabende zu Goethes Geburtstag

A series of plays in the week of Goethe's birthday (28 August), held in Weimar.

September

Winzerfest

Vintners' Festival in Freyburg, East Germany. Many take place around the country at this time of year.

Rhein in Flammen

A spectacular display of ship-launched fireworks all along the Rhine.

Leipziger Musiktage

Music festival in the capital of Sachsen (Saxony).

Oktoberfest

Probably the most famous German festival of all, the Munich beer festival on the Marienwiese sees enormous quantities of beer produced ... and consumed.

Oktober

Bremer Freimarkt

Folk festival in the North German **Hansestadt**.

Hallische Musiktage

Concerts in and around Halle, in Sachsen-Anhalt.

November

Hamburger Dom

Funfair and celebration in Hamburg.

Fest der Freude und des Lichts

Festival of Joy and Light in Schneeberg, in the Erzgebirge on the German-Czech border.

'Es war einmal', or 'Once upon a time': Some common folktales from Germany

As is the case in many countries, it is virtually impossible to be sure of the origins of many of the most popular folktales in the culture. We have already mentioned such works as the epic *Nibelungenlied* in Chapter 3, which can rightfully be called a folk story from the earliest days of the Germanic nations. The Romantic period in Germany saw the first concerted efforts to record what had largely been an oral tradition, with authors like Gottfried Herder bringing out works which claimed various levels of authenticity. One of the best known is *Des Knaben Wunderhorn* (*The Lad's Magical Horn*), published in 1805 by Clemens Brentano and Achim von Arnim. This is a collection of **Volkslieder** (popular, or people's songs) which the friends had collected since their student days, and dedicated to the great Romantic, Goethe.

Die Brüder Grimm

For all the importance of the work by Herder, Brentano and von Arnim, it is impossible to talk about German folktales without mentioning Jakob and Wilhelm Grimm. They were great linguists, fascinated by the early stories of the German peoples, who devoted much of their lives to studying and furthering the German language. They lived and worked in the region of Hessen, and were particularly keen to preserve the many folktales that were told in their region. They interviewed local people, asking them to recount their favourite stories, and, like the Dane Hans Christian Anderssen, recorded many of the world's best-loved folktales. Their two major publications, *Kinder- und Hausmärchen* (*Fairy Tales for Children and the Household*, 1812) and *Deutsche Sagen* (*German Legends*, 1816) were instrumental in creating the great interest in Germany's cultural heritage and the development of the academic disciplines of **Germanistik** and **Volkskunde** (German studies) in German education. A statue of the brothers stands in the town of Hanau, where they were born, and a museum dedicated to their lives can be found in Kassel.

Among many classic stories, the tale of *Rotkäppchen* (*Little Red Riding Hood*) was first written down by the brothers. The story had originated in the woods around Marburg, in Hessen, and the area is still called **Rotkäppchenland** today. Likewise, the famous story of Hansel and Gretel found its roots in the thick woods of that part of Germany. It is no coincidence, surely, that so many German folktales articulate the fear of evils that lurk in the deep, dark forests which covered – and still cover – so much of the land.

Struwwelpeter

The legacy of the Grimms' work has so dominated German culture that only one other popular story from Germany needs mention: *Struwwelpeter*. Like so many of the world's greatest children's stories and folktales, this story was written one Christmas by Heinrich Hoffmann as a present for his son. It is one of a collection of stories written in verse about the misfortunes of various children. But it is the anarchic boy, with his fiery red hair and his long fingernails, who is best remembered. Indeed, *Shock-headed Peter*, as the subsequent English translation called him, came to be exported all round the world. Children loved his stubborn refusal to conform to the expectations of the adult world, and the fact that the first edition of the book, published in 1845, was lavishly illustrated served to make the stories all the more popular.

All of this was, of course, happening at a time when the German people were gradually waking up to the idea of a common national identity. Although these were merely simple children's stories, to read them is to begin to understand what makes **das deutsche Volk** tick ... so don't overlook them in your own studies of Germany and its people!

GLOSSARY

der Feiertag (-e) *public holiday*
es war einmal ... *once upon a time ...*
das Fest (-e) *festival, celebration*

feiern *to celebrate*
das Märchen (-) *fairytale*

Taking it further

To understand better the cultural heritage of German traditions and customs, you can do far worse than to read Grimms' *Fairy Tales*, with many editions available in German and English. A German software company has recently collaborated with the main TV stations to produce the stories as cartoons, which will then also be available on interactive CD-Roms under the title *Simsala Grimm*: expect them to be released in English very soon!

There are a number of useful interactive calendars available on the internet. Try de.calendar.yahoo.com/yc/de for a conventional, German-oriented, calendar and diary. Alternatively, www.uni-bamberg.de/~ballw1/fkal.html is a site listing the exact dates for German moveable feasts 1700–2199, while www.kalendarblatt.de offers a day-by-day mixture of date-related facts, historical events, birthdays and even a 'Quotation of the day'.

For information on regional events and customs try searching specific tourist-board sites using any good search engine.

Beyond that, any reading of German literature or newspapers and magazines will quickly give you a sense of the special events in the lives of Germans, and also of the annual events which mark the passing of the years. If you have satellite TV, and can tune in to the Astra satellite, you will find all the major German TV and radio channels broadcasting in clear signals.

7 | CREATIVITY AND ACHIEVEMENTS IN OTHER SPHERES

Science and technology

In the area of science and technology, Germany has always enjoyed a pre-eminent position in Europe. From the earliest scientist-philosophers to the modern-day engineers and technicians who have ensured that the phrase 'Made in Germany' enjoys worldwide respect, German achievements are many. Between 1900 and 1933, for instance, German scientists were nominated for 31 Nobel awards (the US received just six nominations in the same period), and for quite some time any self-respecting scientist elsewhere in the world made sure that he could read German to enable him to keep abreast of the latest developments.

In the 20th century alone, the names of the most prolific German scientists read like a 'Who's who?' of world science. Wilhelm Röntgen, for instance, received the very first Nobel prize for Physics (in 1901) for his pioneering work in the use of x-rays (x-ray machines are even called *Röntgen-Geräte* in Germany). At the same time Emil von Behring and Robert Koch were winning the battle against tetanus and TB in the field of medicine.

In another area, Heinrich Hertz and Karl Braun were engaged in laying down the principles of radio waves, while Max Planck, Werner Eisenberg and – possibly the best known of all Germany's famous scientists – Albert Einstein led the way in pushing back the frontiers of astronomy, mathematics and astro-physics: they developed quantum theory, quantum mechanics and the theory of relativity respectively.

As the century progressed, Germany also became the centre of another booming industry when Nickolaus Otto and Carl Benz produced their fledgling automobiles. Soon they were joined by

names, and later companies, which are still synonymous with German engineering quality: Gottlieb Daimler, Ferdinand Porsche, Mercedes, BMW, Audi and Volkswagen. In the case of all of these companies, their success in the last 50 years really does speak for itself, and one of Audi's advertising slogans **Vorsprung durch Technik** (advantage through technology) sums up the German ethos in engineering.

Of course, as the 1930s progressed, so the face of German technological research changed. Not only was an increasingly large proportion of Germany's effort put into military rearmament, but, as the Nazi regime tightened its grip on every area of German society, it also saw the mass exodus of countless Jewish scientists and technicians who had been the driving force behind many of Germany's innovations. This didn't stop the process, of course, but the names are fewer and further between, and their achievements are less benign: one interesting example of this phenomenon is the scientist Werner von Braun. He began his career in Germany in the early 1930s, and his pioneering work on rocketry was quickly brought under Nazi control. It was von Braun and his team who developed the notorious V1 self-propelled bombs and 'Doodlebug' rockets which brought so much terror to London in the final years of the war. Following Germany's defeat, however, von Braun quickly found himself in the USA where he made a major contribution to America's Saturn space programme in the 1950s and 1960s.

If we bring this picture right up to date we see that, as well as the successful car manufacturers mentioned earlier, a huge range of

German companies dominate the European, and world, markets: BASF (chemicals), Siemens (computers and electrical goods), Lufthansa (the German airline), to name just a few. Even in the recent economic downturn in Europe these companies have proved themselves to be robust competitors, and lie at the very core of Germany's success over the years.

Food and drink

When it comes to food, certainly, Germany enjoys only limited interest from outsiders. If you were asked to name a German staple food you might come up with **Schwarzwaldtorte** (Black Forest gateau), or one variant of the many German **Würste** (sausages), but the truth is that Germany enjoys a varied and fascinating cuisine. This is partially due to the country's geographical position, lying in the centre of Europe. This has enabled the Germans to enjoy the best of Europe's different national foods, while at the same time allowing them to be adapted subtly to German tastes and requirements. So, for instance, the spicy tastes of Hungarian goulash can be found in many Bavarian dishes, while the distinctive dishes of Eastern Europe are equally at home in Frankfurt an der Oder or Berlin.

Another generalisation is that Germany, with its relatively short coastline and its huge forests, is far less a nation of seafood and more of various game: even quite humble establishments will happily offer venison or boar in various guises, for instance. One thing which can certainly be said is that this meat-rich diet can be quite heavy to the unprepared, so make sure you are ready for this assault on your taste buds if you are going to visit the country. If you are happy to experiment, then you are in for a treat! If you are a vegetarian, however, life can be quite difficult in Germany.

Wollen wir draußen essen? Eating out in Germany

Germans are great fans of eating out, and will do so as often as their budgets allow, it would seem. From the city centre **Imbißständer** (fast-food stalls), where you can grab a **Bratwurst** (fried sausage), **Lebkässemmel** (a kind of pork roll) or piece of pizza, through the half-pub, half-restaurant **Gaststube**, which offers everything from snacks to three-course meals, and on up to the smartest cafes and restaurants of the **Länder** capitals, every man, woman and child loves to sample what is on offer!

Als Vorspeise: For starters

For most Germans, lunch is the main meal of the day, so the starter can be just that, as the prelude to a larger lunch, or it can be an evening snack in its own right. Popular dishes include a whole range of soups, both thin soups with dumplings or meat floating in them and thick **Eintöpfe** (stews), which can be a great winter warmer. Other snacky starters might be **Bratkartoffeln**, which are diced potatoes fried up with **Speck** (thick ham) and paprika; or an imaginative salad, either a **gemischter Salat**, which is a mix of various lettuces and other saladstuffs, or else a salad based around one major ingredient, such as a **Tomatensalat**.

Als Hauptgericht: Main courses

Most main dishes in Germany, whether at home or in a restaurant, are based on meat. And most meat dishes are, in turn, based on **Schweinefleisch** (pork). Although other meats will certainly feature on any respectable menu – principally the game meats of venison, boar and fowl – pork makes up some three-quarters of most Germans' meat intake. Although there are some regional variations in which dish is favourite, they happily wolf down **Schweinehaxen** (pork knuckles) and **Eisbein** (trotters), **Schweinbraten** (roast pork), **Kotelleten** (chops) and **Schnitzel** (escalope or, simply, schnitzel!), and, of course, the ever present **Würste** (sausages) – **Blutwurst**, **Weißwurst**, **Bockwurst**, **Frankfurter** etc. etc. ... the list is seemingly endless, and are all delicious served, as they often are, with a small portion of **Senf** (mustard). One of the most popular daytime snacks is **Currywurst mit Pommes und Mayo** (sausage sprinkled with a mild curry powder, served with french fries and mayonnaise). Surprisingly, beef barely features, even before the BSE scare in Europe in the mid-1990s, and is usually only served as steak. Fish, too, is quite rare, although the north German coastline is clearly the exception here, boasting some fine fish restaurants. As you go further south, however, fish becomes more and more of a delicacy, although the Catholic regions still traditionally eat a fish dish on Fridays, if at all possible.

One pleasant surprise for many visitors is the imaginative way that these dishes tend to be served. Although you will often find just one vegetable accompanying your meal, you will often be given a separate plate of salad to eat. Furthermore, the true revelation is the range of sauces which can cover your order. These can be light and fruity, or thick and powerful, based on wine or even beer, or just a hint of lemon. Many menus seem confusing at first, when several different sorts of **Schnitzel**, for instance, seem to be vying for your attention. In fact, the different names are likely to refer to the different kinds of sauce prepared in that particular establishment, so a **Zigeunerschnitzel** (literally: gypsy schnitzel) will come with the same sauce as the more obvious **Schweinbraten mit Zigeuner-sauce** or **-soße**.

Zum Nachtisch: What's for pudding?

As we have already mentioned, it is in the realm of the sweets and puddings that Germany probably has its best culinary reputation, and with some justification if you are not worried about your waistline. It is here that the German people seem most keen to abide by the maxim '**Man lebt doch nur einmal**' ('You only live once'), and just get on with enjoying themselves. This is nowhere better observed than the four o'clock ritual of **Kaffee und Kuchen** (coffee and cakes), which is religiously observed by families at home, or shoppers in cafes or **Konditoreis**, as often as possible. If you are out, you may select a thick slice of **Käsekuchen** (cheesecake), **Himbeertorte** (raspberry flan) or **Apfelstrudel** (apple pie) from the glass case by the counter and then sit down to enjoy it with your coffee. If that weren't bad enough (from a waistline point of view), you will probably have to ask *not* to have your selection liberally coated in **Schlagsahne** (whipped cream).

Und etwas zum Trinken? Drinks

Although you are as likely to get cola, mineral water, or lemonade in Germany as anywhere else in the world, two drinks dominate the German social scene: wine and beer. Of the two, beer is almost certainly Germany's national drink, with the pro capita consumption of this one drink standing at a staggering 140 litres per person, per year.

It is so important to Germany that the Bavarian army historically put beer at second place in the order of priorities for resupply, just behind ammunition! Technically it was recategorised as a **Lebensmittel** (foodstuff, or, more literally, means of life) to justify this order of priority, but the truth of the matter is that Germans don't really need justification to enjoy their favourite beer.

Beer in Germany is very much a regional affair, but one thing links all the different varieties throughout the country. The **Reinheits-gebot**, Germany's brewing purity law which was passed in the 16th century, forbids the use of any artificial preservatives and is a source of great pride for the breweries. It is one of the few issues to have caused Germany to fall out with the Brussels bureaucrats in recent years, when the European Union suggested that the law was a barrier to free trade and tried to have it abolished. So wherever you go, and whatever you drink, Germans will claim that your beer is actually good for your health! And if you travel around the country, there will be plenty for you to try: famous brands of **Pils** include Becks in the north, Warsteiner and König. In the region around Cologne you will find various **Kölsch** brands, such as Früh and Gaffel. In Berlin you might try a **Weiße**, which is a wheat beer often served with a shot of strawberry sauce, believe it or not. But it is in the south where the range of beers on offer really takes off: most popular are the various Bavarian **Weißbier** or **Weizenbier** which are also wheat beers. Breweries such as Augustiner and Paulaner have produced beer in Munich for centuries, and their **Bierhallen** are packed all day long. Elsewhere you will find heavier **Dunkelbier** (dark beer), **Kristallweizen**, **Altbier** and, strongest of all, **Bock**. Each type is served in its own distinctive glass or tankard, and is as much a part of sampling the delights of a region as is the obligatory photograph in front of a famous landmark!

Wine, too, forms an important part of Germany's cultural life. On the whole, German wines tend to be overshadowed by their French neighbours, and their reputation is hampered by the curious practice of exporting only the sickliest sweet varieties (which the locals, incidentally, refuse to touch). But the various wine-producing areas in Germany are equal to anything in the USA, France or the New World.

The most important wine-growing regions are the Rhein and Mosel valleys, but other centres flourish throughout Germany. Although the Riesling grape is the commonest **Rebsorte**, other grapes are grown, such as the Gewürz-Traminer, the Silvaner and the Müller-Thurgau. The quality of German wines begins with the most basic **Tafelwein** (table wine) or **Qualitätswein** (quality wine), but the quality really gets started when a wine is awarded a certificate from the local vintners' society called a **Prädikat**. The top-notch wines are called **Kabinett**, then **Auslese** (meaning 'picked out') and **Spätlese** (picked late). Finally, the best wines of all are **Eisweine**, which have to be picked when the grapes are still hanging frozen on the vine. A small 0.3 litre bottle of wine can be extremely expensive because **Eiswein** is not produced very often and producing it takes a lot of work. Just like beers, each region has its own distinctive bottle and glasses. Recently, for instance, the Rheingau region (one of the smaller wine-producing areas, on the north bank of the Rhein near Rüdesheim) changed its bottle shape – and colour – in a move which was very controversial at first.

Ausländische Küche: The foreign influence

The cuisines of other cultures have long influenced German cooking, and mention has already been made, for instance, of the import of Hungarian goulash in the south. In more recent years the influences have come from further afar, so if you fancy a change from all the heavy game and rich sauces, you might like to consider going to one of the many Greek restaurants in German towns and cities. Similarly, the large Turkish immigrant population in Germany has given rise to a love of the **Döner Kebap** as a tasty snack, and kiosks can be found in virtually every town and city. Italian cuisine, too, is very popular with Germans, either to sit down and eat in a restaurant, or to enjoy the ubiquitous take-away pizza. Finally, the oriental influence of Chinese food, or more usually Thai or Vietnamese, is growing fast, although almost exclusively in restaurants, and less as take-away.

Media

Das deutsche Kino

Within a few years of the invention of moving pictures, German artists and directors were pumping out films through an exploding network of **Kinos** (cinemas) in the major cities. Although the very first films were often more documentaries (and no less popular for that), it was the boom of the 1920s which saw Weimar Germany's film industry take up a dominant position.

The first classic silent movies to come out of Germany were instilled with the spirit of the Expressionist movement which had swept the art world in the 1920s. The sets of the 1920 film '**Das Kabinett des Doktor Caligari**' ('The Cabinet of Dr Caligari') were very stylised cityscapes, while the storyline of the seductive power of a strong-willed individual over the people has ever since been interpreted as a chilling warning of the rise of the Nazis.

There was nothing that the industry could not do in the Weimar period. Under the leadership of the UFA company, which financed huge, purpose-built film lots at its centre in Babelsberg outside Berlin, the world's blockbusters were churned out with astonishing regularity: Fritz Lang's recreation of the *Nibelungenlied* in the 1924 film '**Siegfried**' necessitated the building of a huge, fully-operational, fire-breathing dragon; the same director's vision of '**Metropolis**' (1927) is still considered a fine example of science fiction; Peter Lorre, the central figure of Lang's '**M: eine Stadt sucht einen Mörder**' ('M: A City searches for a Murderer', 1931), can be regarded as the world's first screen serial murderer, every bit the equal of Anthony Hopkins' Hannibal Lecter in 'The Silence of the Lambs'; and the horror genre was begun by the actor Max Schreck, as the world's first screen vampire in '**Nosferatu**' (directed by F. W. Murnau in 1921). Even when the world of the silent movie gave way to the talkies, the German film industry ensured its success by recording sound tracks in up to four different languages simultaneously.

Weimar decadence

For Germany the 1920s was a strange period, with the austerity and economic hardships of the immediate post-war years combining with a sense of a new social order after the carnage of the trenches. Alongside the new artistic movements of Expressionism and the literary fascination with the **Großstadterfahrung** (experience of the city – see Chapters 4 and 3 respectively) this was a period of liberal values and breaking down of accepted social values: if you have seen Liza Minelli in the film 'Cabaret', you will have a good idea of the atmosphere of the day. In German cinemas this attitude resulted in sexually frank films which challenged and rejected much of society's restricted attitudes. Actresses such as Marlene Dietrich in the film '**Der blaue Engel**' ('The Blue Angel', 1930) or Louise Brooks in '**Die Büchse der Pandora**' ('Pandora's Box', 1928) were the downfall of their bourgeois male protagonists, and both thrilled and revolted audiences in equal measure. But this period of German cinema did not last long, because the same elements which allowed this freedom also contributed to the rise of Hitler and his followers.

Film under the Nazis

Although there had been periods of strict censorship during the Weimar years, this was nothing like the controls now put on film production in Germany. All films had to be approved by the **Reichskulturkammer** (the Party Cultural Chamber), and many of Germany's most talented actors, technicians and directors either chose to go into exile, or were forced to leave, in fear of their lives, many going to America. The 1972 film '**Mephisto**', starring Klaus Maria Brandauer, is a compelling portrayal of the industry in turmoil, and of one actor who chooses to stay and throw in his lot with the Nazis.

It might be something of a surprise to learn that the Nazi film industry was not necessarily dominated by heavy-handed propaganda. Certainly some films did play on the increased atmosphere of anti-Semitism, with '**Jüd Süss**' ('Jew Süss', 1933) being a good example of the pseudo-scientific stereotypes which had long been part of German society. Others appealed to the people's sense of patriotism, or upheld the new **Weltanschauung** of the Nazis: popular 'flicks' such as '**Hitlerjunge Quex**' ('Quex of the Hitler Youth', 1933) portrayed the hero deciding between the left- and right-wing camps. Of course, he rejects the degenerate Communists in favour of the wholesome Nazis. Similarly, the stirring plot of '**Kolberg**' (1945), which showed an old Germanic village holding out against rampaging Slavic hordes, required whole divisions of troops to be pulled out of the eastern front to act as extras.

But most films of the time were aimed solely and shamelessly as entertainment, designed to boost morale and, in later years, to distract the population from the problems of constant setbacks at the front and bombing raids at home: so '**Die Drei von der Tankstelle**' ('The Three from the Petrol Station', 1930) was a charming musical about three young men and their search for love, while '**Münchausen**' (1944) was the very first colour feature in Germany, with fantastic special effects depicting the exploits of the mythical Baron, and is a film which stands up admirably to the version directed by Terry Gilliam 40 years later!

More important, perhaps, is an example of the kind of films that were *not* shown in Nazi Germany. As in other aspects of daily life the authorities were quick to suppress opposition to their methods and aims. So, for instance '**Im Westen nichts Neues**' ('All Quiet on the Western Front', 1930) was quickly banned when the Nazis came to power, for its pacifist tendencies, as was the left-wing proletariat film '**Kuhle Wampe oder wem gehört die Welt?**' ('Kuhle Wampe or To Whom Does the World Belong?', 1932) for its political message. This was, incidentally, directed by Bert Brecht, who quickly fled into exile when the Nazis took control of artistic life in Germany.

Contemporary cinema

The German film industry never regained its glory years after the war. This is not to say that German directors have been absent from world cinema, however. Volker Schlöndorff made his name in the 1970s with a film version of the internationally successful novel '**Die Blechtrommel**' ('Tin Drum', 1979), while the movies of Werner Herzog, such as the 1972 '**Aguirre – der Zorn Gottes**' ('Aguirre – the Wrath of God', with a young Klaus Kinski) enjoyed great critical acclaim. Greater commercial success came to Dorris Dörrie, who has been one of the female directors to come to the fore in the 1970s. Her comedies, such as '**Männer**' ('Men', 1985) and '**Ich und Er**' ('Me and Him', 1987), deal with the complexities of relationships between the sexes, and were huge hits in Germany and Europe. More recently, the young director Sönke Wortmann has been steadily building a huge reputation inside Germany, with a string of successes starting in 1994 with '**Der bewegte Mann**' ('The Emotional Man'), then '**Das Superweib**' ('The Superwoman', 1996), starring Germany's biggest actress, Veronica Ferres. His latest film, '**St Pauli Nacht**' ('St Pauli Night'), based in Hamburg's infamous red light district, is set to become his next hit … already there is talk of Wortmann trying his luck in Hollywood next.

But probably the biggest German hit from a global perspective was Wolfgang Petersen's Second World War submarine thriller '**Das Boot**' ('The Boat', 1982), which presented the unusual perspective of the German side of the war. Interestingly, the biggest U-boat film before had been the nationalistic film '**Morgenrot**' ('Dawn's Red Hue', 1932) which had contained the prophetic words '**Zu leben verstehn wir Deutsche vielleicht schlecht, aber sterben können wir fabelhaft**' ('We Germans don't perhaps know how to live, but we can die brilliantly').

'**Das Boot**' was also a film which projected the captain of the submarine, Jürgen Prochnow, into the world scene. It has to be said that only very few German actors have been able to break into the Hollwood market in the post-war period, with the likes of Prochnow, Max von Sydow, Hanna Schygulla and Marianne Sägebrecht enjoying varying degrees of success. Similarly, only few directors have made any impact on the world scene, and then often only in English-language films. Wim Wenders had a hit with

Film Top 10

All these films are available with English subtitles

'Das Kabinett von Doktor Caligari' – the film which sparked off the Expressionist movement in cinema, and which many consider a premonition of the nation's fascination with strong – even hypnotic – leaders.

'Der letzte Mann' – F.W. Murnau's portrayal of a proud man's decline, which parallels Germany's economic problems in the 1930s.

'Metropolis' – Fritz Lang's classic vision of the future. Thea von Harbou, who plays Maria, was something of a pin-up at the time.

'Die Büchse von Pandora' – A good example of the freedom enjoyed by the German film industry before the Nazis came to power, the sexuality of the lead actress, Louise Brooks, both shocked and thrilled audiences worldwide.

'Die Blechtrommel' – directed by Volker Schlöndorff, this film was, unusually, an international success, and is a fine film version of Günter Grass's classic novel of wartime guilt.

'Die verlorne Ehre der Maria Braun' – another Schlöndorff film, this time a highly critical look at the restrictions placed upon ordinary Germans during the height of the RAF (Rote Armee Faktion) terrorist campaign in the 1970s; also very critical of the role of the press at this time. Stars one of Germany's top female actors, Hanna Schygulla.

'Das Boot' – for many the very best anti-war film of all time, with Jürgen Prochnow as the immutable captain.

'Schtonk' – a genuinely funny look at the scandal of the forged Hitler diaries in the 1980s. The popular Götz George stars as the reporter who first 'discovers' the diaries, with Uwe Ochsenknecht as the forger.

'Hitlerjunge Salomon' – released in English as 'Europa Europa' this is a Holocaust film every bit as moving as Spielberg's 'Schindler's List'. Directed by Agnieszka Holland, the film is a warm, at times amusing portrayal of one young Jew's lucky escape from the camps. It is based on a true story.

'Der geteilte Himmel' – although I have made no reference to the film industry of East Germany before the **Wende**, this film, based on the novel by Christa Wolf, is a fine portrayal of life in the East. It might be difficult to find a copy with subtitles, however.

'Paris, Texas' in 1984, and Percy Adlon's 'Out of Rosenheim' (known in English-speaking countries as 'Baghdad Cafe', 1987) also took good profits from the box office. It is only Wolfgang Petersen who has made a real impact, going on after '**Das Boot**' to direct 'Enemy Mine (1985), 'Shattered' (1990) and 'Outbreak' (1995) in Hollywood. The only other German film project to make an impact worldwide was Edgar Reitz's 15-hour epic '**Heimat**' ('Homeland', 1980–84), which charted the history of one small German village over several generations.

The press: TV and radio

The German broadcasting corporations are divided almost equally between national stations – ARD and ZDF, a regional third channel which is state controlled (Bayern 3, Südwest 3 and so on) and a huge range of private channels such as SAT1, RTL and ARTE. Although the state channels and ARTE try to maintain a stimulating and informative programme, the private satellite stations are almost exclusively filled with American imports, dubbed into German. Since unification all TV channels, unusually, can be received via satellite or cable. This is because the cost of broadcasting to the new **Bundesländer** (those in the former GDR) by conventional means would have been too high. There are currently only very few pay-view stations, for film and top sporting events, but these are bound to increase in number as time goes by.

Popular programmes on German TV include a huge range of home-made soap operas, such as '**Schwarzwaldklinik**' ('Black Forest Clinic'), '**Lindenstraße**', based in a Munich street, or '**Gute Zeiten, Schlechte Zeiten**' ('Good Times, Bad Times'), the longest running soap currently in production. Equally high audiences tune in to the many crime and detective films produced in Germany, with series such as '**Tatort**' ('Crime Scene'), '**Wolffs Revier**' ('Wolff's Beat') and '**Kommissar Beck**' ('Commissioner Beck') being much loved. As far as personalities are concerned, chat shows provide some of Germany's biggest TV stars; Thomas Gottschalk and Margarete Schreinemaker, for instance, have gone on from relatively humble beginnings to become top-earning hosts. Gottschalk also hosts '**Wetten daß?**' ('Do you want to bet?') which is so popular that it recently staged an episode of the challenge show on Mallorca, with a huge live audience of holiday-making Germans.

The main radio stations are also under the control of the regional, third TV stations, and are typically a lively mix of entertainment, news and chat.

The press: Newspapers

As in so many other areas of German life, the printed press tends to be quite regional in its outlook. People like to read their *Wiesbadener Kurier*, say, or the *Berliner Abendzeitung*, which will always include national and international news alongside items of local interest.

Only very few regional papers have become truly national, the biggest being the *Süddeutsche Zeitung*, which is based in Munich, and the *Frankfurter Allgemeine Zeitung*. Both are hefty papers, which lay great worth on their extra sections, called the **Feuilleton**, which cover such topics as economics, travel, literature and computing. Probably most respected of all in this context is the national weekly newspaper, *Die Zeit*, which is a paper aimed solely at the national market. Two other national dailies should be mentioned here, both owned by the Hamburg-based Axel Springer **Verlag**: *Die Welt* is a reasonably serious affair, but the popularist *Bild Zeitung* specialises in sex scandals and outrageous stories. As a consequence it enjoys the highest circulation of any German paper, at 4.5 million copies a day! Heinrich Böll attacked the sensationalism of *Bild*'s journalism in *Die verlorne Ehre der Katharina Blum* (*The Lost Honour of Katharina Blum*, 1974).

The Axel Springer Verlag is also responsible for one of Germany's two weekly news journals, *Stern*. In the post-war period this had a fairly good reputation for serious journalism, but this was probably irreparably damaged in the 1980s when it bought rights to Hitler's war diaries ... which turned out to be forgeries – only after the Verlag had thrown enormous amounts of money after the diaries. The other, far more respectable journal is the *Spiegel* which has a long and respectable tradition. More recently, a new glossy news magazine has come onto the market: *Focus* has made reasonable inroads against the big two, with its advertising slogan of '**Fakten,**

Fakten, **Fakten'**, but it seems unlikely that it will knock either off its top spot in the foreseeable future

Into the future with the Internet

Although the Internet was initially the preserve of English-speaking countries, on the whole, Germany has recently taken to it with relish. A whole range of TV programmes and magazines keep fans up to date with useful web sites and technological advances, and the number of German Internet companies has increased dramatically in recent times. In the world of computers and internet you do not need a great command of the German language: you will find **Computerfreaks** who **surfen im Internet** by the process of **klicken** on their **Maus**.

For someone who wants to keep up with German affairs, of course, the Internet is good news. All the German TV and radio stations have their own sites, as do the majority of the newspapers and magazines, including archived back issues. A list of the most useful is included at the end of this chapter, although the nature of this new and very exciting medium is such that we can't guarantee you will find these sites after a few months!

GLOSSARY

die Wissenschaft (-en) *science*
die Technologie (-n) *technology*
die Industrie (-n) *industry*
der Wissenschaftler (-) / die Wissenschaftlerin (-nen) *scientist*
das Essen / essen *food / to eat*
das Getränk (-e) / trinken *drink / to drink*
das Restaurant (-s) *restaurant*
das Kino (-s) / ins Kino gehen *cinema / to go to the cinema*

der Film (-e) *film*
das Fernsehen *television*
der Rundfunk / das Radio *radio*
der Regisseur (-e) *director / producer*
der Schauspieler (-) / die Schauspielerin (-nen) *actor*
die Presse *press*
die Zeitung (-en) *newspaper*
eine Zeitung kaufen / lesen *to buy / read a newspaper*
die Zeitschrift (-en) *magazine*

Taking it further

Try to catch the few German films which get released overseas, or which are broadcast on television, for an appreciation of the mastery of the early black and white directors, or the fresh approach of today's directors. But when it comes to German food and drink, I'm afraid there's really only one thing to do: get yourself to the country!

Here are some useful web sites you can explore as a starting point for deepening your knowledge of any of the topics covered in this chapter.

Süddeutsche Zeitung at www.sueddeutsche.de
Die Welt at www.welt.de
Bild-Zeitung at www.bild.de
Frankfurter Allgemeine Zeitung at www.faz.de
Focus at www.focus.de
Der Spiegel at www.spiegel.de
Stern at www.stern.de
ARD at www.ard.de
ZDF at www.zdf.de
RTL at www.rtl.de
SAT1 at www.sat1.de

A useful online TV and internet guide can be located at www.tomorrow.de and a very good information and search service is at www.web.de.

Finally, you will find a few typical German recipes at the end of the book, in Appendix B, if you would like to try some of the dishes you might encounter in the country itself.

8 POLITICS IN GERMANY

The political system in Germany today is one of the most successful and stable in Europe; so much so that it is easy to forget the difficulties the country has experienced with democracy in the last 100 years or so. For most of the 18th and 19th centuries democratic reform was slowly and grudgingly granted by the leaders of the various independent states. Indeed, the sequence of confederations and parliaments which were founded and abandoned over the years (see Chapter 1) testify to the lack of division which underpinned the struggle for a single Germany.

Even the **Paulskirche** parliament of 1848, which came together with such high hopes on the part of the liberal reformists, was little more than a pawn in the power struggle then going on between Prussia and Austria. And then there was the ill-fated Weimar democracy, born in chaos and destined to see the rise of the most infamous of dictators, Adolf Hitler.

So when the **Bundesrepublik Deutschland** was founded in 1949 there were plenty of observers ready to predict nothing but difficulties for the latest attempt at democracy in Germany. To their surprise, however, the system went from strength to strength, so that nobody now, with the benefit of hindsight, would ever say that the experiment in democracy which was the Federal Republic was anything but a success. Of course, the collapse of the GDR in 1989 merely reinforced the belief that the West German system had won the ideological battle.

One interesting by-product of the political turmoil seen in Germany over the years is that the German people in general are now very knowledgeable about the political situation in their own country. Not only that, but they are often more clued up about politics in other European countries than the inhabitants themselves! Equally, the turnout at elections is generally 80 per cent or more, even at local level, which is very high for a nation where voting is not a legal requirement.

The Federal Republic of Germany

To trace the developments which led to the Germany of today we need to go back to the vacuum created by the defeat of Nazism in 1945. Germany was divided amongst the Allies into Zones of Occupation, with the USA, Britain and France between them occupying the west of the country, while the Soviet Union controlled the east. Berlin was a special case, and was itself subdivided between the four powers.

When it became clear that ideological differences between the western allies and the Soviet Union were hardening into the Cold War, it was decided in the west to allow western Germany a degree of autonomy. The western **Länder** (federal states) were invited to send representatives to a parliamentary council with the task of drafting a new constitution for the country. It met for the first time on 1 September 1948, chaired by the **Oberbürgermeister** (senior mayor) of Cologne, Konrad Adenauer. By the following May, the council had presented a **Grundgesetz** (literally: basic law) to the western **Länder** for approval, which was duly accepted by 10 of the 11 states under western occupation (interestingly, Bavaria rejected the law on the grounds that it still left too much power in the hands of a central authority, but agreed to abide by the majority decision!). On 23 May 1949, therefore, the **Bundesrepublik Deutschland** was formally inaugurated, although the Allies did not grant the young state total sovereignty until 1955.

Das Grundgesetz: The constitution

The German **Grundgesetz**, as just mentioned, was brought into force on 24 May 1949. The use of the word **Grundgesetz**, meaning 'basic law' was quite deliberate, since it was felt at the time that to call it a **Verfassung** (the German word for constitution) was inappropriate when the state of Germany was divided in two, east and west. It is a measure of the success of this charter that now,°

since reunification has been effected, nobody has suggested that the name be changed! For the purposes of this book, I will mix the terminology by deliberately referring to the **Grundgesetz** as 'constitution', as this is what it really is nowadays.

The task of those members of the working group asked to draft the **Grundgesetz** was enormous: not only were the historical odds piled against them because of the catastrophic experiments in democracy which had gone before, but, far more significantly, they had to ensure that the horrors of the Nazi regime could be avoided in any future government. Moreover, this was the first time in German history that a constitution would be law – other 'parliaments' had made attempts to create a bill of fundamental laws and rights, but these had always been little more than recommendations, and the parliaments' inability to enforce their decrees only served to highlight their ineffectiveness. Now things would be different: under the watchful eyes of the occupying allies, the **Grundgesetz** would bind all citizens, including the law makers themselves.

To this end the men responsible for this job looked to the American Constitution for guidance (Britain does not have a written constitution, so could not be used as a template in this way). The first three articles enshrine the fundamental rights of all human beings to freedom of speech, religion and conscience. Indeed, the next 14 go on to underline this principle, including the right to refuse to fight in the armed forces (**Wehrdienstverweigerung**). These basic rights are unalterable.

Subsequent paragraphs run through the minutiae of a state, outlining principles of education, political life, health and social services. In theory all these laws can be more flexible, and in the years leading up to the present over 100 changes have been made to the text of the German constitution, most recently dealing with the role German armed forces can play in NATO and United Nations peace-keeping missions (see Chapter 12 for more on this subject). Another famous alteration came in the 1970s and 1980s when feminists challenged the right of the constitution to forbid abortion. The social debate about Paragraph 148 (the paragraph in the Constitution dealing with the issue) was intense, and resulted in a challenge to the law being mounted in the **Bundesverfassungsgericht**, the Federal

Constitutional Court (see later), which eventually ruled in favour of a change. By and large, however, the German people are rightly proud of their constitution, and the very fact that debate about its contents does sometimes break out in public life is testimony to the success of that first group's creation.

Das Bund: German federalism

With the current debate about a possible future United States of Europe, federalism is foremost in the minds of many people when they think about politics. Many, particularly within the UK, view European union as some kind of secret German weapon, designed to finish off what Hitler set out to do in 1939. Disregarding official German policy for a moment, most ordinary Germans are actually a little amused, not to say baffled, by British resistance to Europe. They see federalism as a positive thing, with their own country standing as a prime example of how a successful federal system should work.

Die Länder: Nations within a nation

We will begin by looking at the German **Länder**, or states. Since reunification there are 16 of them, and they reflect some of the oldest tribal distinctions within Germany, with identities which sometimes go back over hundreds of years (see box for details). So important are the **Länder** to an understanding of Germany as a whole that it is worth noting that the dying East German regime, in a desperate bid to prop up its perilous position, in 1988/89 reinstated the East German **Länder**, which had officially not existed since 1949. In the end, of course, it did not save them, but it is indicative of the importance of the **Land** in German minds.

From a political point of view, each **Land** has a degree of autonomy which is underlined by the existence of a state parliament, usually (but not always) called the **Landtag**. Local elections, held at least every 4–5 years, give the population of a **Land** a direct say over who is to govern the **Land** over the course of the next electoral period, and are hotly contested by all the major parties. The **Landtag** meets regularly to debate laws and issues relating to that region, and is allowed to pass new laws if they affect only the people over whom they have jurisdiction, and do not in any way

The German *Bundesländer*

	Area (km²)	Population (m)	Capital
Die alten Bundesländer			
Baden-Wurttemberg	35,751	9.6	Stuttgart
Bayern	70,553	11.2	München
Hessen	21,114	5.7	Wiesbaden
Niedersachsen	47,438	7.3	Hannover
Nordrhein-Westfalen	34,068	17.3	Düsseldorf
Rheinland-Pfalz	19,848	3.7	Mainz
Saarland	2,569	1.1	Saarbrücken
Schleswig-Holstein	15,727	2.6	Kiel
Die neuen Bundesländer			
Brandenburg	20,060	2.6	Potsdam
Mecklenburg-Vorpommern	23,835	1.9	Schwerin
Sachsen	18,300	4.8	Dresden
Sachsen-Anhalt	20,445	3.0	Magdeburg
Thüringen	16,251	2.6	Erfurt
Die Städte			
Berlin	883	3.4	—
Bremen	404	0.7	—
Hamburg	755	1.6	—

(Population figures for 1992.)

contravene the **Grundgesetz**. As you can see from the map, the **Länder** are quite large (bigger, for instance, than the counties of Great Britain), so it is not surprising, perhaps, to see the **Landesregierung** (State government) with complete control over, say, road maintenance or childcare provision for working families. What is more surprising, however, is the fact that a **Land** can decide which days should be declared public holidays, or set the school syllabus and examination system, or even raise local taxes to augment local public spending. Finally, and most important here, the **Land** plays a vital role in the next stage of government, the **Bundesrat**.

As part of the **Land** structure, each state parliament elects a leader for the period of its term, known as the **Ministerpräsident** (prime

Germany:
Major cities and Länder

DÄNEMARK

Flensburg
1
Kiel

Lübeck   Rostock
4
Wilhelmshaven   Hamburg   Schwerin   POLAND
Bremen
2   BERLIN
HOLLAND   Wolfsburg   ■ 5
Hanover   Magdeburg   Potsdam   Frankfurt
Braunschweig   an der Oder
3   Münster   Göttingen   6
Dortmund   Halle
Düsseldorf   Wuppertal   Kassel   Erfurt   Leipzig   Dresden
Köln   Weimar   7
Aachen   ■ BONN   9   8
BELGIEN   Frankfurt
am Main
Wiesbaden   DIE
LUXEMBURG   Trier   10   Mainz   Würzburg   TSCHECHISCHE
REPUBLIK
11   Saarbrücken   Nürnberg
Heidelberg
Stuttgart   13
FRANKREICH   12   Augsburg
Freiburg   München   ÖSTERREICH

DIE SCHWEIZ

Länder

0   150 km

1 Schleswig-Holstein
2 Niedersachsen
3 Nordrhein-Westfalen
4 Mecklenburg-Vorpommern
5 Brandenburg

■   National capitals

●   **Land** capitals

○   Other major cities

6 Sachsen-Anhalt
7 Sachsen
8 Thüringen
9 Hessen
10 Rheinland-Pfalz

•••••••••• International boundary

•••••••• Former border between
East and West

------ **Land** borders

11 Saarland
12 Baden-Württemberg
13 Bayern

Note: Hamburg, Bremen and
Berlin are City-Länder

minister). He or she represents the **Landesregierung**, not only within the region, but also at a federal level, so election to the post of **Ministerpräsident** of a **Land** can be an important step for a politician's career.

Der Bundesrat: The federal council

The **Bundesrat**, meaning federal council, is the second chamber in German politics, loosely equating to the British House of Lords, or the American Senate. It is made up of seats which are occupied exclusively by representatives of the **Länder**, on a proportionate basis equal to the number of voters in each **Land**. The job of the **Bundesrat** is straightforward enough: to examine laws passed by parliament and to give its assent if appropriate. It is not uncommon for the **Bundesrat** to be dominated by delegates of a different political persuasion to the majority in the parliament, because voters often protest at **Land** level during the mid-term of a government's period in office. When this happens, it can be harder for the government to pass legislation, but even this is seen as a useful check in the eyes of many Germans, possibly preventing the excesses of a government with dictatorial plans. Finally, the **Minsterpräsidenten** of the various **Länder** take it in turns to assume the presidency of the **Bundesrat**. The incumbent would take control of the country if anything ever happened to the Chancellor.

Der Bundestag: The federal parliament

The highest political institution in Germany, then, is the **Bundestag**, or federal diet (parliament). This body is elected every four years in universal elections for all adults (i.e. aged over 18) in the country. We shall look at how the seats are distributed in a moment, but first it should be pointed out that the role of the **Bundestag** is to elect a government (and thereby a chancellor) based on the votes of the people, to debate and to pass laws. A bill, when introduced, must be read in parliament three times before it can be voted on and, assuming a majority vote is agreed, made law. If the Bill affects the Constitution at all, the law must also gain the assent of the **Bundesrat**.

Voting to the **Bundestag** is by means of a system of personal proportional representation. What this means, in simple terms, is that each voter gets to cast two votes – one for a party, and one for a candidate. Once all these votes (known as the **Erste** and **Zweite Stimme**, or first and second vote) have been counted, half the seats in parliament are allocated to individual candidates in a 'first past the post' fashion, while half are allocated to the parties according to the percentage of votes they receive nationally.

The only restriction placed upon this system is the so-called **Fünf-Prozent-Klausel** (5 per cent hurdle), which only allows parties with a minimum 5 per cent of the national vote to take seats in parliament. Clearly, this is designed to prevent radical parties from gaining a foothold in a small part of the country and then spreading their influence from within parliament, as the Nazis did in the early 1930s.

What all this means in effect is that a candidate may campaign for election in an electoral constituency (**Wahlkreis**) and gain a seat in parliament because he receives a simple majority of the votes cast in that area. But even if he fails to win a seat that way he may well receive one when his party come to allocate seats based on the national proportional vote. Of course, this means that it is practically unheard of for cabinet members of an outgoing, defeated government to end up without a seat on the opposition benches, as occasionally happens in other countries, simply because they lose their constituency seat.

When a politician wins a seat in the **Bundestag**, he or she is known as a **Mitglied des Parlaments** (MdP, member of parliament) and is paid an **Entschädigung** (literally: compensation) to attend parliamentary sessions, employ staff and run constituency matters.

Die Bundesegierung: The government

Once a general election has taken place and the votes have been counted, the overall picture of seats in parliament becomes clear. Thanks to the PR element of elections in Germany, however, that is not the end of the matter. It is virtually impossible for one party to obtain an absolute majority in parliament at this stage, and so the largest party in the elections will begin to negotiate with other, smaller, parties about forming a coalition for the next session of parliament. This can lead to some uneasy alliances, and has even resulted in the 1966 '**Große Koalition**', a grand coalition of all the major parties. Once again, the Germans see this aspect of their system as a particular strength – it is very hard for a single party to gain the lion's share of power, and the smaller coalition member(s) can be an effective brake on the main party's delusions of grandeur. We will return to this aspect of German politics when we examine the individual parties in more detail in the following sections.

Bonn oder Berlin?: The burning issue

We haven't really discussed the 1990 re-unification of Germany here, because it is the bodies and institutions of the western **Bundesrepublik** which 'won' and ousted those of the **Demokratische Republik**. Naturally the new East German **Länder** – still typically referred to as the **neue Bundesländer** (new states), 10 years later – had to be incorporated into the make-up of the **Bundestag**, and so on, but on the whole the takeover, in political terms, was very smooth. In one area of political life, however, the impact of re-unification was huge: the question of Germany's capital and seat of parliament.

When the Allies first considered allowing the two Germanies a degree of self-determination it was quickly agreed that Berlin, the centre of Hitler's **Reich**, should not be the capital any more. From a practical point of view, Berlin was in ruins, and pictures of the **Reichstag** parliament building pocked with bullet holes, and wreathed in smoke, became a potent symbol of Germany's defeat. To that end, the West German capital became Bonn, a small city on the banks of the Rhine, and the new government set up shop there. Although the East German regime promptly named Berlin (East) as its capital and built its parliament there, the **Bundesregierung** met in Bonn throughout the following 40 years. But as soon as the country was re-united the question of Berlin quickly arose. Many felt that Berlin's Nazi (and Communist) associations disqualified it from becoming the capital of the new Germany, but most people were equally dissatisfied with the option of leaving things in Bonn: at the very least, this was seen as a clear signal of 'victory' for the West by people in the former GDR.

After much debate it was decided that Germany's capital would, after all, be Berlin again. Plans were made for the complicated

transfer of power, and the area of the Potsdamer Platz in the centre
of Berlin was earmarked for a new governmental quarter. The area
had been totally bare since the construction of the Berlin Wall in
1961, when it was bulldozed to make a clear fire zone for border
guards, so seemed ideal ... until it was pointed out that the area was
also the site of Hitler's headquarters until 1945. Although building
work continues apace (Berlin is nowadays called Europe's largest
building site), the controversy has not really died away.
Nevertheless, Berlin became the official German capital in 1990,
and the old **Reichstag** building, redesigned by the British architect
Sir Norman Foster, hosted its first full parliamentary session on 19
April 1999.

Der Bundeskanzler: The German Chancellor

The largest party in the aftermath of the elections is invited to form
the government, with its leader elected as the **Bundeskanzler** – the
Chancellor of Germany. There have been just seven Chancellors
since the war, including the current one, Gerhard Schröder, and they
have all come from two of the three main political parties. Again,
because of the need for coalitions in German politics, one of the
first tasks of the Chancellor is to allocate cabinet jobs to members
of both his own party, and of the party or parties which are
supporting the coalition. This process can be a very delicate affair,
and generally takes a few weeks to be fully settled ... after all, a
small party in coalition can just as easily take away its support for
the new government, and thus force a new election, unless it is
suitably rewarded for its loyalty. Chief members of the Chancellor's
new cabinet will be the **Finanzminister** (finance minister), the
Verteidigungsminister (defence minister) and the **Außenminister**

German **Bundeskanzler** since the war	
1949 Konrad Adenauer (CDU)	1974 Helmut Schmidt (SPD)
	1982 Helmut Kohl (CDU)
1963 Ludwig Erhard (CDU)	1998 Gerhard Schröder (SPD)
1966 Kurt Kiesinger (CDU)	
1969 Willy Brandt (SPD)	

(foreign minister). These posts will go to senior members of the Chancellor's own party, as well as the leader and other senior members of the coalition party. In this way it is highly likely that a member of a small political party in Germany can hold a position of real power, even if his party will never stand a chance of winning the majority of votes in an election.

As well as presiding over his cabinet, and the parliament, the **Bundeskanzler** is, of course, the main representative of Germany overseas. Even if his foreign minister does all the spadework, it is the Chancellor who will stand in front of the press cameras when the next European treaty is signed, and for many Germans this aspect of his role is probably even more important than how he performs at home. Despite his success, many were horrified by Helmut Kohl's image overseas, for instance, and especially that he could not speak English when dealing with foreign representatives.

Der Bundespräsident: Federal president, the nation's figurehead

The **Bundespräsident** is the representative head of state in Germany, but the office is severely restricted when compared to pre-war presidents, who enjoyed too much power and were very difficult to restrain by parliament. Nowadays, therefore, his role is purely ceremonial, with the important exception that he, at the Chancellor's request, dissolves parliament following a successful vote of no-confidence in the Chancellor (known as a **Mißtrauensvotum**). Otherwise, the most important role of the President is as a non-political representative of his country in the wider world. Certainly a previous incumbent, Richard von Weizsäcker, gained international respect for his sensitive approach to the issue of German war guilt.

German **Bundespräsidenten** since 1945

1949	Theodor Heuss (FDP)	1979	Karl Carstens (CDU)
1959	Heinrich Lübke (CDU)	1984	Richard von Weizsäcker (CDU)
1969	Gustav Heinemann (SPD)	1994	Roman Herzog (SPD)
1974	Walter Scheel (FDP)	1999	Johannes Rau (SPD)

The **Bundespräsident** is elected at a special assembly, known as the **Bundesversammlung**, which is the only time that **Bundestag** and **Länder**-appointed **Bundesrat** deputies meet together. A successful candidate holds the post for five years, and may be re-elected only once. Interestingly, although there is an element of party politics involved in this election, this is less apparent than in other areas of political life, and the President is expected to act in a largely apolitical way once elected.

Das Bundesverfassungsgericht: The constitutional court

The last institution of Federal Germany which needs to be examined is the **Bundesverfassungsgericht**, which is the constitutional court. This body is unique to post-war Germany, and was called into being specifically to avoid the abuses of the law perpetrated by successive governments in the past. It has its seat in Karlsruhe in Baden-Württemberg, and consists of eight federal judges whose task is to ensure that any proposed new laws are legal under the terms of the Constitution.

Another important aspect of the Court is to act as a safeguard to the democratic principles of the country, by examining the aims of every political party active in the public sphere. If the court deems a party's aims to be unconstitutional, i.e. acting against the fundamental rights of freedom of speech, religion, etc., then it can take the ultimate action of declaring the party illegal: this has, in fact, happened several times over the years, including the banning of the Communist Party during the Cold War (somewhat controversially) and more recently, of a number of Neo-Nazi parties.

Finally, the **Bundesverfassungsgericht** can stand as the ultimate adjudicator between any two parties in a legal dispute, whether they be individual citizens, a company or even a **Land**. The appearance of the judges in their rich red robes, to utter judgement on a particular case, is always avidly reported by the country's media and invariably generates great public interest.

Die Parteien: Political parties

 CDU/CSU

Arguably the most important party in modern German politics, the **Christlich-Demokratische Union** (CDU, Christian Democratic Union) has held power more often than any other post-war party. This is a right-of-centre group which, as its name suggests, claims to hold conservative, Christian values as the centre of its beliefs.

In Bayern the CDU does not field candidates in elections, because it is allied to a smaller party, the **Christlich-Soziale Union** (CSU, Christian Social Union) which is exclusively Bavarian.

The first **Bundeskanzler**, Konrad Adenauer (1949–1963), was a CDU leader, while Helmut Kohl (1982–1998) held office for longer even than Bismarck did in the 19th century – too long according to many when he lost spectacularly in the 1998 general election. Despite his rather ignominious ending and a subsequent scandal concerning shady dealings over party funds, he will always be remembered as the Chancellor who brought about the re-unification of Germany in 1989.

 SPD

One of the mistakes which allowed the Nazis to gain power in the 1930s was the lack of unity between the various left-wing parties of the Weimar Republic. The **Sozialdemokratische Partei Deutschlands** (SPD, Social Democratic Party of Germany), which is the inheritor of the many pre-war goups, nowadays aims to present a united front. It has been the second most successful political party in post-war German politics, and currently holds the majority in the **Bundestag** with its leader, Gerhard Schröder, the current **Bundeskanzler**.

Willy Brandt (1969–1974) is remembered as the SPD Chancellor who believed passionately in improving West Germany's relationship with the GDR and other Soviet bloc neighbours. This came to be known as his **Ostpolitik** (Eastern politics) and culminated in his gesture of kneeling, hand in hand with the Polish

President, in the pouring rain in front of a memorial to the Warsaw ghetto.

FDP

The **Freie Demokratische Partei** (FDP, Free Democratic Party) is Germany's liberal party. It is the FDP which typically has held the balance of power when majority parties have been seeking to create a working government after general elections, even though it has never won an election or had a chancellor in parliament. Nevertheless, the FDP has enjoyed a level of influence which would have been impossible in other countries with different electoral systems. The threat of withdrawing support from a creaking majority has been used as a powerful weapon, and the FDP has gone as far as forcing new elections on a few occasions. In recent years its influence has, however, waned with the emergence of other minority parties. One FDP MP of great international standing in recent years was Hansdietrich Genscher, who was Kohl's Foreign Minister at the time of reunification.

Bündnis 90/Die Grünen

When the Green movement began to mobilise in the 1970s observers gave them little chance of catching the public imagination, much less of coming to play any kind of influential role in European politics. But in Germany, under the charismatic (and controversial) leadership of Petra Kelly and others, this is exactly what the German Greens did. In 1983, when the first Green MPs entered the parliamentary chamber in jeans and sweatshirts, they caused outrage among the established parties, but were seen as a refreshing change by the electorate. Their influence was greatly enhanced after the **Wende** when the eastern Greens, known as **Bündnis 90** (Alliance 90), joined the main party. After a number of important successes at local and European elections, they polled enough votes in the 1998 general election to enter into government for the first time, supporting the SPD majority in coalition. Nowadays their biggest crisis is that most of their candidates have matured into middle age, and have needed to redefine their 'student generation' image a little! The current Party leader, Joska Fischer, is Germany's Foreign Minister at the time of writing.

PDS

This is one of the newest German parties, having been formed from the demoralised remnants of the Communist organ in the former GDR, the **Sozialistische Einheits- partei** (SED, Social Unity Party). The **Partei Demokratischer Sozialisten** (PDS, Party of Democratic Socialists) was, of course, as good as dead in the first years after unification. It has, however, enjoyed a steady revival of its fortunes in recent years, particularly in the East, as voters became disillusioned with the seemingly hollow promises of the then CDU government. The change of government to Schröder's SPD, itself left of centre, has done little to reverse this trend. For a while in 1998 it looked like the SPD might have formed a 'red coalition' with the Communists, which is a measure of how far they have come in just one decade. The Party is currently lead by the charismatic Gregor Gysi, who has been a contributory factor in the Party's revived fortunes.

Die Republikaner

Finally it is necessary to look briefly at the **Republikaner** (known colloquially as **Die Reps**, the Republicans), which is Germany's only legal right-wing party. Although they are careful to avoid the wrath of the **Bundesverfassunsgericht**, their manifesto is still pretty distasteful, preaching a mixture of extreme patriotism with anti-European and anti-foreigner rhetoric. Periodically they make small gains in one region or another, which invariably causes an element of panic among the mainstream parties, but to date this has largely been due to short-lived protest voting. It should not be forgotten, however, that many pundits similarly dismissed the **Nationalsozialistische Deutsche Arbeiter Partei** (NSDAP, Nationalist Socialist German Workers' Party) as an irrelevance, along with its leader, Adolf Hitler...

GLOSSARY

die Politik *politics*
der Politiker (-) die Politikerin (-nen)
  politician
Mitglied des Parlaments (MdP)
  member of parliament

die Stimme (-n) *vote*
die Wahl (-en) *vote, election*
der Wähler (-) die Wählerin (-nen)
  voter
die Partei (-en) *Party*

Taking it further

There are a number of books which go into the German political system in more detail: one is John Ardagh's *Germany and the Germans* (1987, reprinted 1995), but the *Dictionary of Contemporary Germany* (edited by Tristram Carrington-Windo and Katrin Kohl, 1999) also contains useful entries for the major parties and institutions. Another source of up-to-date information is, of course, the Internet. The web sites of the major parties, as well as the German government itself, are:

federal government web pages at www.bundesregierung.de
web site of the incumbent president at www.bundespraesident.de.

The major political Parties can be found at the following sites:
www.spd.de
www.cdu.de
www.liberale.de
www.gruene.de
www.pdsnetz.de.

Finally, you might like to use the Internet to find out about the individual **Bundesländer**. Generally, you should type in www.[name of the state].de, remembering that e.g. **ü** should be replaced by ue. Also, the on-line brochure www.bundesregierung. de/tatsachen_ueber_deutschland contains a wealth of information about the **Länder**, the government, landscape, industry, etc. It is also available as a printed booklet and is updated every year or so.

9 | THE BASICS FOR LIVING

In this chapter we will cover some aspects of daily life which don't perhaps fit easily into some of the categories discussed so far: education, transport, health care and so on.

Education

Germany developed an education system very early, even by European standards. What is more surprising is that the system was developing even before the country had been properly united for the first time: as we have seen in previous chapters, some German universities, for instance, are very old indeed.

The benefits of this tradition are plain to see. Much of Germany's technological achievement and the nation's prosperity are thanks to the fact that a large proportion of her citizens attend some form of education for many years.

The education system is nowadays under federal control, with the government making recommendations which are then interpreted by the individual **Länder** as each sees fit. This allows a great deal of flexibility from **Land** to **Land**, while ensuring high standards throughout the country.

Der erste Schritt – Kindergarten: The first step

A German's education usually begins at **Kindergarten**, which typically begins at the age of three. This is voluntary, but statistics show that some 80 per cent of German children (66,000 in 1985) attend either a morning group, or all day. Although the emphasis is very much on fun, all activities have an educational value and, moreover, the classes instill a sense of discipline and learning which will be so important to the child for many years. Evidence of the success of this system is the fact that the very name, **Kindergarten** (meaning 'children's garden', by the way), is now applied to pre-school clubs in many countries of the world, even if they are not German speaking.

Primärstufe: Primary education

From the age of six, education is compulsory for German children until they reach 16. All children, therefore, attend **Grundschule** for four years. Subjects studied include basic mathematics, **Mathe**, science, **Wissenschaft** and geography, **Erdkunde**, as well as German, of course.

Sekundärstufe: Secondary education

At the secondary level German youngsters find themselves streamed for the first time, according to ability. Although the principles of a **Gesamtschulausbildung** (comprehensive education) have made inroads into education policy in recent decades, it is more common for a child to be sent to a school appropriate to his or her ability.

Hauptschule

This is a secondary school for ages 10–15. The majority of the young people who attend are likely to go on to vocational training at a **Berufsschule**.

Realschule

Here, too, courses are offered until the age of 15 or 16, but these students will sit an academic examination at the end of their courses called the **mittlere Reife** or **mittlerer Abschluß**, a mid-term matriculation. This qualification allows a student to switch to further academic or vocational courses.

Fachschule

The **Fachschulen** were developed for post-16 education with a definite vocational leaning. This allows young people to train for middle management posts, for instance.

Gymnasium

These schools are considered the academic elite at secondary level, offering academic instruction right through to the age of 19, at which time students sit their university matriculation examinations, called **Abitur**. They cover a range of subjects, in a complex combination of majors and subsidiaries. Certain subjects, such as mathematics and a foreign language, are compulsory. Although they receive a mark from 1 (called **sehr gut** – very good) to 6 (**ungenügend** – unsatisfactory) in each subject, students and their parents are only really interested in the **Notendurchschnitt** (average score). An average of 4.0 is the minimum pass mark, and determines whether a student gets into university or not.

Die Hochschulen: Higher and further education

Any student who holds a pass mark at **Abitur** is entitled to a university place. Here, too, the student can follow a number of different routes depending on subject.

Universität

German universities still maintain the principles of a pure, academic education, although this is not to say that their courses have not evolved over the years. Alongside the traditional (and very popular) disciplines of, say **Germanistik** (German studies) or **Philosophie**, **Chemie** (chemistry) or **Medizin**, courses such as **Jura** (law) and, particularly, **Betriebswirtschaftlehre** (business and economic studies, otherwise known as BWL to most German students), have become extremely popular. Some of these subjects might require attendance at a **technische Hochschule**, but the system is similar in both institutions.

Courses are offered on a semester basis, with first degrees lasting anything up to six years or longer, at the end of which successful candidates will be awarded their **Magister**, or (depending on discipline) a **Diplom** or **Staatsexamen** qualification. Although those that reach this stage are generally very well educated, the fall-out rate along the way can be brutally high, especially in the more competitive fields. But this does not seem to have deterred Germany's youth: from a figure of 6 per cent in 1950, more than

20 per cent of young people attend a higher education institution nowadays. A fairly large number go on to PhD level, too, gaining their **Promotion** if successful.

Of course, there are some drawbacks to the system. Firstly, studying at a German university is horrendously expensive. Technically the least well off are eligible for BAFöG (a state loan, which stands for **Bundesausbildungsförderungsgesetz**, if you must know!), but the reality is that very few are awarded this assistance. There is also a real problem of overcrowding nowadays in a system which has barely expanded at all to meet the post-war boom in demand. Some courses now operate a *numerus clausus* system, whereby numbers are set at the beginning of a semester, but this is having little impact. Finally, the average time to complete a first degree at a German university is extremely long, standing at five to six years, depending on the subject (philosophy is the worst, at fourteen semesters – seven years). Proposals by some universities to introduce compulsory final examinations at the end of, say, eight semesters have been fiercely resisted by students, but they may have to wake up to the reality that Germany produces some of the oldest graduates in Europe.

Health

Health provision in Germany is of a very high standard, with the population getting high quality care from the moment they are born until the very end of their lives. This was always meant to be a fundamental part of the **Sozialstaat** conceived by the founders of the **Bundesrepublik** in the 1940s, and the system has worked very well ever since. The fact that the system is also largely privately run has not held the Germans back, either, although we shall return to some pitfalls in a little while.

One of the consequences of the private system is that there are a bewildering number of insurance companies (known as **Krankenkassen** or illness funds), health clinic consortia and hospital administrators. Even the ambulances are run by a range of companies, although they do at least tend to look the same, painted in cream and dayglo red! The larger insurance companies, such as the AOK, offer their clients far more than just health insurance, however, and play a huge part in the lives of the vast majority of Germans.

Health insurance is not cheap, which means that German doctors and hospitals are amongst the best equipped in the world. The national ratio of patients to doctors is also very good, standing at approximately 1:400. But this also means that German people are keen to ensure they get their money's worth, and as a consequence they are quick to consult their doctors whenever they are ill – and insist on the best treatment while they are at it! To the outsider it can sometimes seem that the Germans are virtually a nation of hypochondriacs, because they are always interested in health issues, but really it is just a case of knowing what is owed them.

Even when they are not ill, the Germans seem to spend a lot of their time making sure that they do not fall ill: spa resorts (any town with a **Bad** in its name is technically a spa) are hugely popular, and many insurance schemes allow their clients to claim one spa holiday every year. So they might go to Bad Aibling, in Bavaria, to be immersed in the peat baths there, or drink the rather evil-smelling waters of Wiesbaden. They might just spend the time at a health farm, engaging in swimming, cycling or rambling. Even the people who do not go to these lengths may well choose instead to read up on alternative, homeopathic medicines. They will buy healthy food and useful herbs from their local **Reformhaus** (health food shop), or ask for **Bio-Obst** (organic fruit) from their greengrocer.

Health concerns in Germany

Two major health issues in Germany in recent years have, in fact, been global issues. Both drug use and the spread of AIDS engaged the attentions of the German health service more and more towards the end of the 20th century. The government has devoted a great deal of effort and expenditure to trying to prevent these problems, with intensive advertising on television and in the press. Sports stars and other celebrities have been drafted in to press home the two slogans at the centre of the campaigns **'Gib' AIDS keine Chance'** (Don't give AIDS a chance') or **'Keine Macht den Drogen'** ('No power to drugs'). It is hard to say whether these campaigns have had any real effect, but certainly neither problem has yet been eradicated.

The biggest problem of all, however, stems from the fact that Germany, like most western nations, is increasingly a country of old people. The **Sozialnetz** (social net), which supports those who cannot help themselves, is becoming increasingly stretched as more and more people live to a greater age and require longer periods of care. The German government has already admitted that the current system will not be able to carry the burden for much longer, and people will be facing some hard decisions in the next few years. At the moment there is fierce opposition to the proposed solution of raised taxes to cover the deficit, but the problem will not go away. Add to this the current debate about the continuation of national service (many young German men opt to do a social posting called **Zivildienst** (civil service) instead of joining the military, which is very useful for hospitals etc.) and it is clear to see that the German health service has some tough times ahead.

Housing

First impressions of German housing are that standards are very high, although the former-GDR **Länder** are generally behind the West. Certainly it is true that the standards expected of any new buildings are among the highest in Europe. Almost every aspect of house building is covered by one piece of legislation or another: triple glazing is prescribed, for instance, as are the build quality of every internal door, electric socket and the thickness of the sound

and heat insulation between the walls. Even the **Trabantenstädte**, the commuter townships built on the outskirts of Munich, Düsseldorf or Rostock, can boast incredibly comfortable buildings, even if many Germans consider them poor.

Of course the picture in the East is different, because the government has inherited the legacy of the huge concrete high-rise monstrosities built by the East German regime in the 1950s and 1960s, to counter the extreme housing shortage there after the war. Although there are plans to knock these down eventually and replace them with better housing, it seems certain that they will be a feature of the skyline for many years yet. Some tower blocks in the West have come to be regarded as eyesores over the years, too, but once again they are at least built to a relatively high standard.

Even if we take a look at older, more traditional regions, such as deepest Swabia, or some of the villages of Hessen, the picture-postcard exteriors can be deceptive. Step inside the hallway of these houses and it quickly becomes apparent that a lot of money has been spent on these properties over the years. It may look old from the outside, but the inside is likely to boast all mod-cons and a level of luxuriousness which astonishes.

One phenomenon which had a major effect on the shape of housing in the cities was the bombing in the final months of the Second World War. Some cities were virtually flattened by the Allied raids, which has meant that they had to be rebuilt, almost brick by brick, in the late 1940s. As ever, the innovative Germans did not merely rebuild what had been there before, but instead chose to improve things for their fellow citizens. Small blocks of apartments typically boast a sheltered courtyard for parking or for the families in that block to play in. Even larger blocks will have underground parking and cellars for people to store their winter tyres and their skis, and all those other things that normally clutter up a crowded flat.

Significantly, perhaps, the proportion of home ownership in Germany is extremely low. Mortgages (**Hypotheken**) are available, but house prices are very high, even by the German wage standards, and mortgages can be very expensive to obtain. There would seem to be a Catch-22 operating here, too, because house prices are kept high in a small market, and for as long as people choose to rent or lease a house, the cost of buying is bound to stay high. So most Germans will go through their entire lives only dreaming of owning their own home, and if they do manage to buy you can be fairly sure that they will never try to move house again.

What this all means is that the German population is not particularly mobile. Although you will always find exceptions, it seems that most Germans are still quite content to live and work in the region where they were born, and many would consider a move to a different **Land** unthinkable, unless they had no family ties back home. Some areas, particularly the high-tech capital of Munich, see a greater level of movement, but others can have several generations of the same family living in the same village, with the one brother or nephew who has moved 20 kilometres away being considered something of a black sheep! Incidentally, such families are likely to inherit a house from their parents or grandparents, which is another reason why they are then 'tied' to the area.

So what kind of things do you have to take into consideration if you want to rent a small apartment in a major German city? You might first go to an **Immobilienmakler** to find the right property. These will have a database of houses and apartments on the market, and will try to match you to the right place. This service is not cheap, however, sometimes costing as much as a whole month's rent if you decide to take the flat.

Miete (rent) in Germany is invariably calculated on a square metre basis, and most Germans will tell you that they live in a $12m^2$ flat, rather than tell you the number of bedrooms etc. You also have to ask whether the advertised rent is **warm** (with electricity and other facilities included in the price) or **kalt**. Once you decide to take the property, you will be asked to pay a month's **Kaution** (key money), but thereafter you will not usually be bothered by your landlord. One of the advantages of the rent market being so large is that there are lots of laws designed to prevent abuse of the landlord–tenant relationship, and if you need to report a fault you will find it is dealt with pretty quickly. Equally significant is the fact that a contract is binding for as long as the tenant chooses, and cannot easily be terminated by the landlord on a whim. Nevertheless, most Germans who are in such an apartment long for the day when they will possess the keys to their own home, not least because they would love to change things around and laze in a garden (rare in city blocks, of course). This is one reason why German cities are often ringed by **Schrebergärten**, which are like large allotment gardens, divided into modest plots. A family will build a small shack on their land, and will spend many of their weekends out there, maybe even sleeping over when the city becomes too hot in the summer, enjoying their little holiday.

Love thy neighbour?

One final consideration if you are thinking about going to live in Germany is the bureaucracy which surrounds even this most basic of social requirements. A German's home might well be his castle, but he is not as free to behave as he likes therein as you might think. Whole volumes of German law are devoted to a householder's (or tenant's) duties, and to those activities from which he must abstain. So, for instance, he will be required to sweep the path in front of his house clear of leaves, snow and ice every morning in the autumn and winter. In an apartment he will have to join the rota to ensure that the block has fulfilled its collective obligations. Added to this is legislation about when he is allowed to wash his car, when he may or may not play his stereo above a certain volume, and even a total ban on those noisy do-it-yourself jobs during the weekend. You might be imagining that people probably don't take these laws too seriously (after all, virtually every council in the world has such bye-laws). But the German people can be very litigious, and spend no end of time and money in the local courts each year, locked in battle with their neigbours over the seemingly most trivial disputes … only the lawyers are happy about this aspect of living in Germany!

Transport

Being such a large area of land, transport is a major concern, with the car being king in German society. But allied to this fact it is also pertinent to point out that Germany has one of the most advanced public transport systems in the world. However you choose to do it, if you need to get from, say, Munich to Hamburg in a hurry, you can be sure that your journey will be smooth and your arrival (probably) punctual!

Cars

If there were one cliché to which most non-Germans would subscribe about daily life in Germany it would be the image of the fat Mercedes cruising down the **Autobahn** at 200kph. From a figure of 11 cars per 1000 population in 1950, car ownership has boomed in Germany. Nowadays the figure is approaching 500/1000 – nearly one car per two members of the population. The German people are rightly proud of their national car manufacturers, and typically will only buy from VW, Porsche, Audi, BMW, Opel or Mercedes-Benz. They are also proud of the extended network of motorways, with over 10,000km criss-crossing the country, second only to the USA. And yes, there are some stretches of German motorway where there is an unlimited speed restriction, but the large numbers of cars on the roads today mean that it is increasingly difficult to go faster than the 40kph that is usually reached at all the roadworks and traffic jams which snarl up the modern network.

Autokennzeichen: Spot the number plate

A	Augsburg	HB	(Hansestadt) Bremen	P	Potsdam
B	Berlin	HH	(Hansestadt) Hamburg	PA	Passau
BN	Bonn	HL	(Hansestadt) Lübeck	PB	Paderborn
C	Chemnitz	HRO	(Hansestadt) Rostock	R	Regensburg
D	Düsseldorf	J	Jena	S	Stuttgart
DA	Darmstadt	K	Köln	TR	Trier
DD	Dresden	KI	Kiel	TÜ	Tübingen
DO	Dortmund	L	Leipzig	UL	Ulm
E	Essen	M	München	W	Wuppertal
F	Frankfurt am Main	MA	Mannheim	WI	Wiesbaden
FF	Frankfurt an der Oder	MD	Magdeburg	WO	Worms
FR	Freiburg	MZ	Mainz	WÜ	Würzburg
H	Hannover	N	Nürnberg	Z	Zwickau

You might have noticed that, in general, the larger cities use fewer letters. 'Guess the city' is a fun game which can while away the hours on a German **Autobahn**! Note, though, that this box contains only a few of the commonest you will see.

To keep your car on the road in Germany you will first have to go to the **Zulassungsstelle** (registration office) in the local area to provide evidence of ownership and insurance cover. You will then be issued with a number plate which shows the area of registration (see box). If you move house, you will be required to re-register your car in your new area. You will also have to make sure that your car passes its **TÜV-Prüfung** (a legal car-safety test) before you can take it out onto the road. But once you get there, a car is relatively cheap to run: fuel costs are low, by European standards, and road tax is calculated on engine size, which is good news for smaller, more economical cars.

Staying on the right side of the law

Despite the lack of a speed limit on some motorways, German laws relating to driving are typically complex. The main sanction which can be applied to a driver is the loss of points on his licence, and the offences related to this punishment are wide. Some are quite obvious, such as speeding or drink driving, but some can be quite bizarre (even if applied for good reason). If it can be proved that you were driving too close to the car in front of you, for instance, you will suffer quite serious consequences, although this does not stop the practice of 'tailgating' when a large BMW wants to get past you on the motorway.

Alkohol am Steuer: Drink driving

As far as drink driving is concerned, you can be punished by law if you cause an accident and are found to have 0.3 parts per million (ppm) of alcohol in your bloodstream, although this level is not an offence in itself. From 0.5 ppm, however, you can be stopped and arrested even if you have committed no other offence, although the punishment is relatively light. But by the time you are found to have 0.8 ppm in your blood, the consequence is an immediate **Fahrverbot** (temporary driving ban) for one month, a fine of DM500 and four points on your driving licence. If you are caught with more than 1.1 ppm alcohol in your blood, you will be fined a large sum and lose your licence entirely (called **Entziehung der Fahrerlaubnis**) and you might even be jailed. Periodically the government even considers the zero tolerance option with regard to alcohol at the wheel, but this has recently been rejected, once again, as impractical.

All fines, punishments and points are recorded at the **Verkehrszentralregister** (Central Traffic Register) in Flensburg, north Germany. Many people who lose their licence for a period of time are required to attend a course in good driving, and often also a **medizinisch-psychologische Untersuchung** (medical-psychological examination, known by many Germans as the **Idiotentest**) before they are allowed to drive again.

Another Michael Schumacher

From the one extreme of unlimited speed, most German motorways actually have a speed limit of 120kph, reduced to 100kph when the motorway goes through built-up areas, or is approaching a complex junction. On the **Bundestraßen**, the main regional routes, the limit is always 100kph, and this drops automatically to 50kph once you reach the yellow **Ortsschilder** at the outskirts of every city, town or village. Inside the town the limit can drop to 30kph, or even 20kph where children might be playing. Of course, plenty of people choose to ignore these limits, but be warned: the German police can be quite sneaky with their speed traps. Most Germans accept that they will be caught periodically by a hidden camera, although the penalties for, say, 10kph over the limit are quite light anyway, consisting of a small on-the-spot fine, called **Bußgeld** or **Verwarnungsgeld** depending on the offence.

Die grüne Welle and das grüne Pfeil

Two things that you should take into account when driving in German involve the colour green. No, this is not a reference to an environmentally friendly fuel available at German filling stations, but rather two signs designed to keep traffic moving inside cities and towns. The **grüne Welle** (green wave) is a series of interlinked traffic lights which are synchronised to guarantee a driver greens all along the route if he drives at the displayed speed limit, and is very useful in a congested urban area. If you are the impatient type who always zooms off at the lights you will quickly grow very frustrated, because you will simply catch up with the red lights at every junction. If, however, you are happy to cruise along at 40kph, then you will literally 'surf' through the town on a wave of green lights. Very useful! The **grünes Pfeil** (green arrow), however, has been a little more controversial. It is one of the very few things to have been adopted by the whole of Germany after the **Wende** (reunification), which originated in the GDR. The idea is that a junction controlled by traffic lights might display a sign with a green arrow pointing right. If you see one of these you are supposed to turn right even if the traffic lights show red! You have to give way to any pedestrians who might be crossing, of course, but if you hesitate you are likely to get a blast from the horn of the car driver behind. West Germans were rather reluctant to accept this road traffic measure at first, but the evidence of accident statistics would seem to suggest that drivers have more or less got used to the idea in the interim.

Öffentliche Verkehrsmittel: Public transport

Despite the popularity of the private car, German people are generally quite happy to turn to the public transport network for some of their journeys. This is mainly because the system is so good: somehow you get the feeling that German people simply wouldn't tolerate late trains and dirty buses. Let's have a look at some of the transport systems available.

Inter-regional travel

If you want to get quickly from one German city to another, and you don't want the stress of the high-speed **Autobahn**, then you have two main choices. If you want to fly, you will find that Germany has an excellent network of airports, with every medium sized and large city offering a small airport (many of them even have limited international flights). The really big ones, at Frankfurt, Munich and Berlin, are then fed by all the smaller ones, so the network can be very convenient indeed, especially for businessmen who want to complete the very long north-south journeys that are possible within Germany's borders.

But most people choose to go by train if they have to get to a different German city. **Die Bahn** (the railway, a renamed amalgamation of the West German **Bundesbahn** and East German **Reichsbahn**) is a private company which presides over an enormous network of tracks covering the entire country down to quite rural levels. It has managed to run this network for several decades now with an incredibly high level of efficiency, punctuality and cleanliness envied by rail systems around Europe and the world. When the company began services with its prestigious **ICE** trains (standing, in fact, for Inter-City Express – very German!), things seemed to be getting still better. Typical journey times, even before the **ICE**s began, were Hamburg to Munich in six hours, and the price was very competitive. But in recent years standards have begun to slip, and a number of highly publicised accidents, including the **ICE** disaster at Eschede in October 1998 where 80 people died, have begun to raise doubts over the long-term future of **Die Bahn**. A survey of 1999 showed 39 per cent of customers were 'dissatisfied' with the service, double the figure for 1998. Despite TV adverts directed by the famous German film maker Wim Wenders, confidence continues to fall.

Despite these problems, train travel in Germany remains a quick, efficient and enjoyable experience. Plans to improve the service have included a proposed **Transrapid Schwebebahn** monorail link between Hamburg and Berlin (which has fallen into financial and technological difficulties in recent years), and a new luxury train called the **Metropolitan**, costing DM55 million, between Hamburg and Cologne. This train, which went into service in the summer of 1999, has luxury seating, wooden tables, conference rooms and computer terminals on board, and offers a standard of service to rival that of the airlines.

Regional travel

Where the German rail system really comes into its own is for those short journeys which feed into the local town or city. For years now most German cities have been surrounded by a radiating network of **S-Bahn** routes. These specially built trains run quickly and fairly quietly between the citycentre and the outlying towns and villages, with a service which peaks at some 4–5 trains an hour (in both directions) and runs for some 20 hours a day. For many commuters and shoppers, faced with the hellish prospect of fighting for an expensive parking space, the **S-Bahn** is the only kind of transport worth considering. In recent years the principle has been extended to offer **Inter-Regio** trains which shuttle between selected neighbouring cities, and these have proved equally popular.

Inside towns and cities

And then there is the question of moving around within Germany's major towns and cities. Here, three systems have been deliberately integrated to provide a very reasonable public transport system. Whether you travel by **U-Bahn** (underground), **Bus** or **Straßenbahn** (tram), you will usually find that your ticket is valid for all three modes of transport, that your connections will link seamlessly, and that each system operates quickly and smoothly. Although not spotlessly clean, the underground stations are tidy and totally unthreatening environments, the trams a real picture as they snake along the cobbled streets, and the buses very paragons of both passenger- and environment-friendly transport. If you are visiting a city for a short period you will find that one of the 24-hour tickets will be an absolute godsend as you jump from bus, to tram, to underground, and back onto a bus.

While on this point, it is usually pointed out that the German city transport systems are very easy to fiddle. It is true that you alone are responsible for stamping your ticket as you climb on board. It is also true that many people consider the fine, should you be caught, to be worth the overall savings made. But it is especially embarrassing to have a whole carriage of travellers stare at you as the controller explains to you, in perfect English, that your excuse does not interest him and you have to pay …

So those are some of the basics for living in Germany, but of course there are many others that we could have mentioned here: the recycling craze, 'green' Germany, problems with bureaucracy. Some of them we will come to in other chapters, but let me close this chapter by saying that time spent in Germany is rarely wasted, and German people who recognise that you are making an effort to integrate will be truly delighted to help you along. Don't be afraid, dive in!

GLOSSARY

die Ausbildung *education*
die Schule (-n) *school*
zur Schule gehen *to go to school*
der Schüler (-) / die Schülerin (-nen)
  pupil
der Student (-en) / die Studentin
  (-nen) *student*
die Gesundheit *health*
krank sein *to be ill*
der Arzt (Ärzte) / die Ärztin (-nen)
  doctor
das Krankenhaus (-häuser) *hospital*
die Apotheke (-n) *chemist*
das Haus (Häuser) *house*
die Wohnung (-en) *flat*

wohnen *to live*
zu Hause *at home*
der Verkehr *traffic*
das Auto (-s) *car*
der Bus (-se) *bus*
die Straßenbahn (-en) *tram*
die Bahn (-en) / der Zug (Züge)
  railway / train
das Flugzeug (-e) *aeroplane*
fahren *to go, ride*
reisen *to travel*
fliegen *to fly*
mit dem Auto / mit der Bahn
  by car / train
schwarz fahren *to travel without a
  valid ticket*

Taking it further

The information in this chapter, perhaps more than anywhere else, is best confirmed by personal, hands-on experience of life in Germany and contact with German people. So go on: try learning German, read some books and, when you get the chance, visit Germany yourself. You won't be disappointed!

10 THE GERMANS AT WORK AND PLAY

There is little doubt that the Germans are a very hard-working people. After all, the nation's post-war prosperity has been built upon the principles of hard work and high quality. What is perhaps more surprising is that they like to play just as much: sporting activities, cultural pursuits, games and just socialising with friends and relatives all form a large part of the lives of most German people. But how do they divide their day? What constitutes work, and what counts as play?

The Germans at work

Economic reconstruction

Bearing in mind that Germany lay in ruins in 1945 it is astonishing to think that she has been the single largest economic power in post-war Europe. Ironically the Allies' intention at the 1945 Yalta Conference was to impose conditions on Germany which would ensure she could never again threaten European stability. So what happened to change all this?

A major factor was the Cold War. By the time the two German states were founded in 1949 they had been fully integrated into NATO and the European Community, on the one side, and the Warsaw Pact on the other. The Marshall Plan, like the Dawes Plan in the First World War, was an economic aid package put together by the USA to allow the whole of Europe to rebuild quickly, ready to fight a new war against the East.

But another factor in Germany's recovery, which cannot be overlooked, was the willingness of the population to put the horrors of the war behind them. The **Trümmerfrauen** (rubble women) set the tone by reconstructing the destroyed cities by hand. Thanks to their hard work, mostly without the help of the male population (the last German POWs only returned from the Soviet Union in 1957), Germany rose from the ashes.

Following this physical reconstruction, West Germany then experienced its **Wirtschaftswunder** (economic miracle). Under the guidance of Chancellor Adenauer's economics minister, Ludwig Erhard, production rose, unemployment fell, and the nation began to enjoy increasing wealth. With the founding of the independent **Bundesbank** (Federal Bank) in 1957, the gross national product more than doubled in the following decade (to DM 458,200 in 1965). It is important to recognise that this boom was only possible because of the unique level of cooperation which existed between Germany's main industries, the unions and the financial authorities.

Trade relations

Unions had been banned under the Nazis, so they were quite deliberately a vital part of post-war rebuilding. Throughout the world, industrial relations in Germany have been applauded as the epitome of a progressive, modern state. Instead of the normal animosity which tends to exist between workforce and management, and which has plagued western nations for years, German trades unions have enjoyed a high level of **Mitbestimmung** (joint decision making) in the post-war period.

Negotiations between workers and their managers have been aided by the shape of trades unions in Germany. These are large, single-interest bodies representing all workers in one sector. Typical **Gewerkschaften** (unions) include the **Gewerkschaft Öffentliche Dienste, Transport und Verkehr** (ÖTV, the transport union) or **IG-Metall** (the union of the steel industry). In return for their virtual monopoly in each sector, the unions agreed a system of collective bargaining known as the **Tarifvertrag**, which makes any agreement concluded between workforce and management legally binding. Crucially, strikes during or after such bargaining are then illegal, as are strikes which are deemed to be purely politically motivated; even then, a vote of 75 per cent of the workforce is required in a secret ballot to authorise strike action. What this all means is that trade relations have been extremely good, with the biggest problems in the 1980s resulting from negotiations over a shorter working week.

The social state

The German social state has traditionally been the envy of the world. Healthcare, although privately funded, is also heavily subsidised by the government (see Chapter 9), while unemployment has been a major priority for all post-war governments. Mindful of the ease with which the Nazis manipulated the appalling unemployment rates of the Weimar period, unemployment has generally been low, while the levels of **Arbeitslosengeld** (unemployment benefit) have been extremely generous (between 53–60 per cent of previous net pay). However, reunification and a slow-down in the European economy, coupled with the prospect of a demographically older population, has led to worries that the state can no longer afford to maintain the current level of state support.

Apprenticeships

Another area which has been very successful in post-war Germany has been the programme to ensure that the majority of young people coming onto the market are well qualified for a particular trade or profession. We have already looked at the education system in some detail in Chapter 9, but here it is worth mentioning the 300+ **Ausbildungsberufe** (literally: training professions) recognised by the government. These are state-sponsored apprenticeships which consist of a guaranteed training place with a master craftsman, plus paid vocational training. Crucially, this has ensured that young **Auszubildender** (**Azubis**, or apprentices) enjoy a good level of respect among the population at large, and the scheme is extremely successful. A young man or woman will tell you with evident pride when he or she has gained a **Lehre** place, often using this, older, term to describe their apprenticeship.

Perks and benefits

What all these measures add up to is a favourable working environment, with a generally happy workforce. We have already pointed out the benefits to the country as a whole, but the fact that Germans are prepared to work loyally, and for long hours, has also resulted in great benefits for them, too. Despite the fact that a German will commonly work from 7.00am to 5.00pm during the week, it is also common for them to finish at midday every Friday, and to enjoy very generous holiday allowances.

Then there is the much-coveted **Dreizehntes Monatsgehalt** (13th monthly pay packet) – an extra month's tax-free pay, which is paid to many workers, typically as a Christmas bonus. This, too, is disappearing fast as economic hardships bite.

1990s – the bubble bursts

During the 1980s it seemed as if there were nothing that the West German economy could not achieve. So when the East German government began to collapse in 1989, and reunification seemed imminent, Chancellor Helmut Kohl confidently announced that it would not cost a Pfennig to the West German taxpayer. East German citizens were granted 40 Marks each as a forerunner to full monetary unification in 1990, and the country was ecstatic at the ease with which full reunification was achieved.

But in the following months and years it became obvious that Kohl's confidence was misplaced. As the full scale of East Germany's economic troubles came to light, the German government announced a new tax, known as the **Solidaritätszuschlag** (solidarity supplement). This can amount to as much of 7.5 per cent of a western family's taxable income (lower for poorer households, and for people in the former East), and has been incredibly unpopular. Although Kohl's government easily won the election immediately following reunification, mounting economic troubles and a big increase in unemployment in the early 1990s resulted in dissatisfaction throughout the country, but particularly in the **neue Bundesländer** (the former DDR-**Länder**).

New measures

When Gerhard Schröder became the new **Bundeskanzler** (federal chancellor) in 1998, he and his SPD party pledged to overhaul the troubled welfare state in Germany. It was obvious that the system then operating in Germany was a child of the **Wirtschaftswunder** of the 1960s and 1970s. Although the generally good relations between unions and management had enabled Germany to avoid the recessions of the late 1980s, by the 1990s there were real fears for the country's economic prospects. Despite the concerns of the population (who, quite naturally, feared a watering down of their rights and privileges) and fierce opposition from the unions, it became all too clear that the German **Sozialstaat** was no longer viable. Tough measures would be necessary before the ageing population in Germany made the state bankrupt.

At the time of writing, the Government was still examining ways to save money in virtually every area of public life in Germany. The **Sparpaket** (package of savings measures) proposed by the **Finanzminister** (finance minister) Hans Eichel in 1999 examines transport, state pensions, healthcare, taxation levels and so on, in great detail. Although many expected Schröder's SPD to be less left wing than traditionally, there has been surprise – and some approval – expressed at the reforms proposed. Although it is hard to say what form things will eventually take, it seems likely that the system will change. Harder still to predict is whether the generally good working conditions which German workers have enjoyed in the post-war years can be maintained, or whether they will have to work longer hours, for less money, to keep the country afloat.

The Germans at play

As well as working hard, however, the Germans like to play hard, too. Partly as a result of what is for many a long working day, German people enjoy more holiday time than most Europeans (not forgetting the many public holidays discussed in Chapter 6). All in all, your average German worker can expect to have as many as 45–50 days off each year. Indeed, a staggering 65 per cent of the population enjoy six weeks or more holiday each year. A respectable 29 per cent more make do with five weeks!

For schoolchildren, too, finding activities to fill in their time after school is very important. Most pupils finish school at lunch, and although they will certainly have homework to do, there is still plenty of time left in which they can get bored!

So what kind of things does the typical German family get up to in the afternoon, or evening? What games do they play? What do they talk about? Perhaps it comes as no surprise, but television is an increasingly dominant factor in most families. With most households having access to cable or satellite, and so many channels to choose from, viewing times have risen dramatically in the last few decades. The figure is, however, lower than in many other countries, and demonstrates that the art of entertainment within the family is not dead!

Some traditional games

One piece of evidence which supports the belief that Germans enjoy their own company in the evening is the popularity of card and board games in toyshops there. One very old card game which enjoys undiminished popularity nowadays is '**Skat**'. It uses a modified pack of cards, and many traditional designs of cards are sold. '**Skat**' has deceptively simple rules, which belie the difficult tactics necessary to become a champion player. Another traditional tabletop game, which originated in the 1920s, is '**Tipp-Fußball**'. It is a simplified football game with a hexagonal ball and model players whose legs kick when a button is pressed on their heads! It is played with fanatical devotion by youngsters and adults alike, and many regions have their own leagues and cup competitions, with an annual nationwide cup. If the whole family want to play a game, then '**Mensch, ärgere dich nicht**' (literally: 'Don't get worked up, man', the German game of 'Ludo') or '**Halma**' (a game which involves moving around a board capturing the opponents' hats) are still very popular. Significantly, the German '**Spiel des Jahres**' (game of the year) prize is a significant event which usually sees the winner sold out for many weeks: recent winners have included '**Die Siedler von Catan**' ('The Settlers of Catan') in 1995, which encourages players to collect natural resources, trade with opponents and gradually colonise an island, and '**Mississippi Queen**', the 1997 winner, which sees small paddle steamers racing along a river to be the first to pick up passengers. It is a shame that these games only rarely make the breakthrough to sales outside of Germany.

The rise of the PC

One possible threat to the traditional board game in Germany is the arrival of the home computer. Although they have been slower to bring PCs into the home, the Germans are now enthusiastic fans, and computer games are becoming ever more popular. What is rather sad, however, is that the vast majority of the games sold in Germany for computers are the standard US and British blockbusters – 'Tomb Raider', 'Civilization', 'Theme Park' – with very few home-produced software packages enjoying any success. Although it is perhaps too early to suggest that the computer game will oust the board game entirely in the years to come, concern is being voiced in the press about the trend.

Cultural Activities

For many Germans, a little free time means a chance to indulge in their favourite cultural pastime. With no one city dominating the scene in the way that London or Paris perhaps do in their countries, every German city can offer a wide range of museums, galleries and theatres to suit every taste. The combination of high-quality events and a cheap and convenient public transport system means that an evening out in Munich, Stuttgart or Frankfurt is a popular option, and in the summertime especially, families will enjoy a meal, a play and a few hours in a warm **Biergarten** on a pretty regular basis. Similarly, most municipal authorities provide a range of open-air concerts, plays and even films in their parks and town squares throughout the warmer months.

The importance of membership

Many of the activities already mentioned here will take place under the auspices of a **Verein**, or association. **Vereine** are a large and important part of German cultural life, with as many as one in three Germans belonging to one. The range of such organisations is quite vast, with the most popular being **Sängervereine** (choirs), **Sportvereine** (sports associations) and **Schützenvereine** (sharp-shooting clubs). Some 2 million Germans are members of organised choirs alone, and the rifle clubs play a very important role in many communities, especially in the south, where they will form honour guards at local fetes and undertake very popular open days every year. They will almost certainly also enjoy their own **Stammtisch** (literally: regular table) at a local **Kneipe** or **Gasthof**, and will rather conveniently hold all their committee meetings there! Even more novel is the central importance of the **freiwillige Feuerwehr**, the volunteer fire service, which can be found in many areas: not only do these men and women provide a useful service for places which might otherwise have no such security, but they are hugely popular as social groups too. Equally useful to some young men is the fact that service in the local volunteer fire brigade unit may exempt them from national service.

Youth Organisations

For younger people there is also the option of joining a **Jugendverein**, although these hold a less important place in German cultural life than in other countries. The main reason for this is the lingering distrust of uniformed organisations in Germany, inherited from the Nazis' use of the **Hitlerjugend** and **Bund Deutscher Mädels** (the boys' and girls' Nazi youth movements), and the virtually compulsory membership of the **Freie Deutsche Jugend** (Free German Youth) in the former GDR. Virtually the only acceptable uniformed organisation nowadays is the **Pfadfinder** (scout movement) which recruits boys and girls alike. Significantly, most scout groups have virtually no uniform to speak of, and place great emphasis upon the mutual notions of brotherhood and individualism. In many ways the movement has inherited the mantle of the **Wandervögel**, a bohemian travelling movement popular in the 1920s, which itself took its roots from the practice of the travelling artisan apprentice of previous centuries. Some scout groups are affiliated to the churches, and they alone add the element of Christian teaching, as you would expect. Indeed, it is the churches which offer almost the only other organised youth work in the shape of the normal youth clubs common to most cultures.

Sports in Germany

We have already mentioned the popularity of the **Sportvereine** in Germany. Sport is the unchallenged number one favourite activity, whether by participation or as a spectator. Indeed, during the Cold War the two Germanies (fortunately) fought their ideological battles on the sportsfield as an alternative to physically fighting. This had the knock-on effect of causing huge amounts of money to be spent on facilities for both populations, and vast coverage in the media of every success, worldwide, regardless of the sport involved. In the 1960s and 1970s, the West German government spent nearly 20 million Marks on football stadia, tennis clubs, swimming pools and the like, and the nation is still reaping the benefit today. The **Deutscher Sportbund** (DSB, German Sports Federation) nowadays oversees virtually all sporting activity in Germany, and their periodic campaigns to encourage yet more people into active participation are invariably successful.

The most popular sport by far is soccer. Although the German education system is less likely to see pupils playing in school teams, local leagues for town and village teams are common and the big cities can have several leagues, all feeding talent into the national **Bundesligen** (federal leagues). At this level, German teams are very successful, and most people outside Germany will have heard of teams like Bayern München, FC Köln, Schalke 04 or Borussia Mönchengladbach. These teams, in turn, have provided players who have brought success to the national side in many of the post-war World Cup competitions: indeed, the 1954 World Cup final victory of West Germany over a much fancied Hungarian team did a great deal to restore the badly battered pride of a nation still struggling to recover from the privations of the war. Over the years, Franz Beckenbauer, Karlheinz Rummenigge, Lothar Mathias and Jürgen Klinsmann have been feted as world-class players and have won virtually every honour available.

A range of sports vie for second spot in the popularity stakes. As far as team games are concerned, handball is common, as is ice hockey in the winter season. More recently American gridiron football has gained a wide following, with a large number of exotically-named teams participating in national and European leagues. Popular individual sports include tennis, with the massive success of Steffi Graf and Boris Becker in the 1980s and early 1990s making a huge impact, and the seasonal winter sports of skiing and snowboarding. Most Germans, not just those who live near the Alps, grow up with regular skiing holidays, and even the older generation will maintain their fitness in the winter by following well-marked cross-country ski routes. In this sport in particular, a healthy rivalry with the other German-speaking Alpine nations means that a steady flow of potential new World Champions is guaranteed. Finally, the success of Michael Schumacher in recent years has seen a steady growth in interest in Formula 1 motor racing, although exclusively in the realm of a spectator sport, it has to be said!

Holidays

Finally we turn to the issue of holidays. As we have already mentioned, the German people tend to take more, and longer, holidays than any other nation in Europe. Indeed, it has been said that the Germans spend more money on holidays than any other nation on earth, including the Americans. Of course, the holidays they choose to go on are many and varied, but certain trends are quite apparent.

Home is where the heart is

For many families a holiday 'at home' is a logical option. Germany is such a large country, and grew even larger in 1989 for a generation which knew nothing about the 'other' Germany on the opposite side of the Iron Curtain. From the rugged coastline of the Baltic, to the breathtaking rock formations of the **Sächsische Schweiz** (Saxon Switzerland), the romance of the Rhine and the majesty of the Alps, for many an exploration of their own country is both fascinating, and relatively cheap. According to a recent survey, more than one-third of Germans choose this option every year, although they may enjoy a trip abroad in the same year, too.

One fascinating problem which has arisen since reunification has been the issue of nude sunbathing in Germany! Although a modest percentage of West Germans have always enjoyed stripping naked on the Baltic coast in the summertime, for East Germans under the Communist regime it was almost *de rigeur* to bathe in the nude. This habit was in response to a freedom rarely granted them in other aspects of their lives. Now, in the years following the fall of the Wall, West German tourists are complaining about the levels of nudity they experience when visiting the coastline of East Germany. The East Germans, on the other hand, see this as just another example of the West imposing its values on the East, and are fighting for their right to strip! Although this might seem quite amusing to an outsider, it is a serious reflection of the tensions which have arisen between the two since unification, not to mention an indication of how seriously all Germans take their holiday-making.

Mallorca-Reisen

When it comes to choosing a destination for a holiday, many German families still want nothing more than a flight to the sun. By far and away the most popular resort for such a holiday is the Mediterranean island of Mallorca, or the **Putzfraueninsel** (cleaning ladies' island) as some Germans derogatorily call it. Each year Germans pile onto charter planes to the island and then soak up the sun's rays on the beach, just a few short paces from bars, restaurants and shops offering **Weißbier**, **Sauerkraut** and the *Bild-Zeitung*. In 1998 the figure was an astonishing 3.5 million, which is more than one-third of all the tourists who visited the island: one MP courted controversy in 1994 when he suggested that Mallorca was actually the 14th **Bundesland**! The fact that the likes of Boris Becker and Claudia Schiffer have chosen to buy villas on the island has only served to increase the island's popularity.

It is in places like Mallorca that Germans have earned their reputation for being jealous hoarders of the hotel's sunloungers, getting up hours before any one else to claim their territory. And if you think that we are succumbing to a mild, but not insignificant, piece of racism, let me assure you that many Germans are equally aware of – and deeply ashamed of – their compatriots' behaviour!

Moving further afield

Certainly it is true to say that the German people are keen travellers. They are avid fans of the English-speaking countries, but also love to visit the countries closest to them, with the Czech Republic, Hungary and Poland immensely popular nowadays. But above all else, the Germans have traditionally been adventurous travellers, second only to the real experts of Australia and New Zealand. Surveys have shown that as many as one in five Germans prefer to choose an activity holiday above all else: you will see them trekking across the Sahara on camels, paddling down the Orinoco river or fishing through small holes cut into the Arctic pack ice. Once they get the urge to go, no venture is too daunting for them, it seems!

The Germans at work and play

Whatever else may be said about the Germans when at work, or relaxing, one thing remains true: both aspects of their lives are worthy of their full attention and all their efforts. It can be no coincidence that one of the most powerful and hard-working industrial nations has also produced so many world-beating teams and sportspeople. As the European nations move closer together, with Germany apparently driving the pace of the union, you have to wonder whether the German workforce will share its love of leisure activities as generously as its loyalty and conscientious nature. If it does, then Europe could become a very interesting place indeed!

GLOSSARY

die Arbeit *work*
der Arbeitsgeber (-)/der Arbeitsnehmer (-) *employer/employee*
arbeiten *to work*
die Firma (-en) *company*
AG, Aktiengesellschaft *Plc*
GmbH, Gesellschaft mit beschränkter Haftung *Ltd*

der Arbeitstag (-e) *working day*
der Feierabend *end of working day*
das Wochenende (-n) *weekend*
die Freizeit *spare time*
das Hobby (-s) *hobby*
das Brettspiel (-e) *board game*
das Computerspiel (-e) *computer game*
das Kartenspiel (-e) *card game*
die Ferien (pl) *(school etc.) holidays*
im Urlaub *on holiday*

Taking it further

Much that has been written about working conditions in Germany is quite heavy going, but you might like to read Stuart Parkes' interesting work *Understanding Contemporary Germany* (Routledge, 1997). Alternatively, the major periodicals, ***Spiegel*** and ***Focus*** for instance, publish regular articles on the state of the nation's economy and workplace.

As has been mentioned in this chapter, many of Germany's most popular games are not readily available overseas, but specialist games shops often import a few copies, if there is the demand. Keep a look out for any of the '**Spiel des Jahres**' stickers on the boxes, because you cannot go far wrong with any of them – even those which were shortlisted, or only win the silver prize.

As far as German **Vereine** are concerned, many now have their own web sites on the Net, but it is not possible to provide a complete list here. Try www.[name of organisation].de, remembering that letters with umlauts have to be replaced by e.g. **ae** (for ä).

For a light-hearted and frank portrayal of the Mallorca syndrome, you could do worse than to see the film, '**Ballermann 6**', a comedy based around a famous German bar and nightclub on Mallorca.

11 | THE GERMAN PEOPLE

So far we have looked at many aspects of German life and culture, all of which have an effect on the people who live in the country. But what of the people themselves? What is **der Durchschnittsmensch** (the average German man or woman) like? Indeed, is it possible to draw any 'typical' picture at all, in a country which still retains its strong regional characteristics?

Some German stereotypes

It might be worthwhile first of all examining a few of the stereotypes which exist about the German people, just to see whether there is any validity at all in any of them. What do people think that Germans are like, before they meet any of them?

All Germans wear Lederhosen and swig beer

This is one of many stereotypes which actually derive from a particular region of Germany – in this case from **Bayern** (Bavaria). It is true that some Bavarians still dress in their traditional costumes for special events, and it is certainly true to say that many Germans drink a lot of beer (see Chapter 6 if you have forgotten just how much).

The Germans are a militaristic race

Again there is an element of truth contained in this cliché, but really it is an historical truth. Clearly much of Germany's history has been dominated by their aggressive expansionism; indeed, Germany might never have united had it not been for the highly militarised Prussians. But if we look at today's Germans, then this stereotype certainly no longer applies. If anything, the majority of Germans

nowadays are very pacifist, as evidenced by the response to the crises in Yugoslavia in the late 1990s. More on this issue in Chapter 12.

Humour does not exist in Germany

This particular cliché highlights perfectly how difficult it is for different cultures to interact. Of course Germans have a healthy sense of humour, it's just that it tends to be different from the Anglo-Saxon sense of humour: where an American is amused by sarcasm, the German is amused by satire; where the Briton laughs at clever word plays, the German laughs at slapstick. Humour is alive and well in Germany, but you need a better understanding of the culture in general before you can really appreciate it. One particularly rich vein of jokes in recent years has been the difficult transition from a divided country to a united nation. Many West Germans have enjoyed jokes at the expense of the (apparently) less-sophisticated former GDR citizens, poking fun at their inability to obtain 'exotic' fruits such as bananas during the GDR days, for instance.

Don't forget, also, that cabaret – an entertainment form virtually invented, and certainly perfected, in inter-war Germany – centres on political satire and a very sophisticated form of humour.

The Germans are a cold and unfriendly race

This cliché could not be further from the truth, but has arisen because visitors to the country only ever see the public face of Germans. In contrast to Anglo-Saxon countries, where new relationships tend to begin in a fairly informal way, Germans make a much more distinct division between their public and private lives. This is reinforced by the language itself, which uses different modes of address for strangers and respected colleagues, and members of the family and the close circle of friends. More on this later.

Demographics

Population trends

Since reunification, the population of Germany has been a little over 80 million people (82 million in 1996), but since 1974 the number has been in gradual decline, because Germany has had the lowest birthrate in the world. Although there was a mini-boom immediately after reunification, the worry that '**Die Deutschen sterben aus**' ('The Germans are dying out') is still reflected in the media from time to time. Of course, this is a trend which can be observed in virtually all countries in the so-called 'First World', but it is no less worrying to the German people for that.

Minority populations

Germany, too, has some sizeable minority populations. Ironically, these minorities seem to have no problems maintaining a very healthy birthrate, which has served to fuel fears among right wingers that the native population is being squeezed out (see the section on racism later in this chapter). Of course, when you look at the figures for these communities, such worries are unjustified, but they persist nonetheless.

The Turkish community is the largest in Germany, standing at some 2.04 million in the late 1990s. Turks are often referred to as **Gastarbeiter** (guest workers), reflecting the initial reason for them settling in Germany in the 1960s and 1970s. Almost every city in the west of Germany now has a Turkish area, and the children of these communities can be second- or even third-generation German born. Up to now, these children have had no right to German nationality, even though many feel as much German as Turk. There have been moves to change this ruling, pushed particularly by the

Green Party (**Bündnis 90/Die Grünen**) since it began to share power with Gerhard Schröder's SPD in 1998. The plight of the Turks was first highlighted by the author Günter Wallraff, who published an account of life as a Turkish factory worker in 1985, called *Ganz unten* (*Right at the Bottom*).

While Germany was still divided, the Socialist regime in East Germany agreed to take large numbers of Vietnamese refugees (as a show of solidarity with the Communist government there). In the **neue Bundesländer**, therefore, there are large communities of Vietnamese, and some can be found in the western cities too.

Finally, it is worth noting that Germany has received far more refugees from the conflicts which have dogged the Balkans in the 1990s. This is partly due to a sense of responsibility for actions committed by Germany in that region in the Second World War, but also reflects the relative economic strength of Germany within Europe nowadays (this issue is looked at in more detail in Chapter 12). Since the first fighting in the region, Germany has granted asylum to nearly 2 million citizens from the various states of former Yugoslavia.

Young and old in Germany

As well as resulting in a declining population, the low birthrate in Germany also means that the population consists increasingly of older people. A graph showing the age structure of a 'healthy' population (meaning one which is renewing itself and expanding at average rates) should always show a rough pyramid, with the oldest age category (90–100 years old) being the smallest. In recent years, however, Germany's age pyramid has shown signs of turning upside down, with more and more people surviving into old age, but fewer and fewer babies being born to give the pyramid a large base. As has been discussed in previous chapters, this phenomenon is already causing problems for welfare provision – a shrinking group at working age is paying for the pensions and healthcare of a growing elderly population. This is bound to have great economic and social implications in the years to come.

Popular names

Vornamen

So what are common names in Germany? Of course, the choice of popular **Vornamen** (first names) can be highly influenced by short-lived fashions, or world events, but for what it is worth, here is a chart of the commonest names given to babies in 1994.

Most popular names for new babies during 1994

Girls	(West)	(East)	Boys	(West)	(East)
1.	Julia	Lisa	1.	Alexander	Philipp
2.	Katharina	Maria	2.	Daniel	Maximilian
3.	Maria	Julia	3.	Maximilian	Paul
4.	Laura	Anne/Anna	4.	Christian	Kevin
5.	Anna	Sarah	5.	Lukas	Sebastian

It is interesting to note that there is a reasonable overlap between the top girls' names in the east and west of Germany, but less so with boys' names (although there is more overlap evident if we were to look at the top ten). Also significant is that many of the 'traditional' German names, such as Wolfgang, Günter or Volker for boys, Hannelore or Beate for girls, are falling out of use. What isn't apparent from these lists is the increasing popularity of foreign names for German children, especially French and English names. It is not at all uncommon nowadays to be introduced to a Renée, Sandrine, Tommy or Steve, even if the spellings can be a little unusual at times!

Nachnamen/Familiennamen

As far as **Nachnamen** (surnames) are concerned, some of the commonest are those of the traditional craftsmen who adopted their trades as their surnames in medieval times: Müller (miller), Schmidt (smith), Schneider (tailor), Zimmermann (carpenter), but equally common can be Maier, Hoffmann, Braun (Brown) or Weiss (White). Thanks to earlier 'colonial' contacts, Slavic names are also surprisingly common.

Terms of address

One feature that will certainly present itself early on in any stay in Germany is the greater use of titles and surnames. In most of English-speaking countries we are used to introducing ourselves simply as 'John Smith', and usually expect people to address us with our first name from an early stage in our relationships. In Germany this is very rare: although the habit is changing among younger Germans, most people prefer to be addressed by their title, plus their surname. Indeed, many Germans introduce themselves with a brusque-sounding 'Schmidt' (or whatever), as they shake your hand, so that you don't know their first name at all. Henceforth, you would call that man simply 'Herr Schmidt' or a woman 'Frau Schneider', sometimes for years. In addition, if someone has a professional title, this will usually feature too: 'Herr Doktor Schwarz', 'Frau Ingenieur Müller' etc. Sometimes the title replaces a name altogether, so that the German chancellor is often addressed as 'Herr Bundeskanzler' alone.

The social role of *du/Sie*

There is an important linguistic reason for this custom just outlined: unlike English speakers, Germans have to choose between two forms of 'you'. **Du** and (its plural form **ihr**), which corresponds to the rather old-fashioned English 'thou', are reserved exclusively for use in the family, with close friends and children, and with pets (but also with God!). It is also normal to use first names when you are on **du** terms with someone. Nowadays younger people (it is hard to define exactly what age we are talking about here, but up to mid- to late-twenties, perhaps) often use **du** when they first meet each other socially, but at work would still address a new colleague of the same age with **Sie**. From this you will see that it is not appropriate to address a German stranger with the **du** form; you should instead use the formal equivalent, **Sie**. Equally, it would be quite rude to use someone's first name while still on **Sie** terms. You will find details of the differences between the verb forms of these modes of address in any good grammar book, but you can see a few examples in the box.

Du and *Sie* forms	
du bist	thou art (informal)
Sie sind	you are (formal)
du hast	thou hast
Sie haben	you have

Switching from *Sie* to *du*

At this stage you might think that you will never get to know a German well enough to want to switch to **du**. You might, equally, be thinking that it all sounds so complicated that you never want to have to worry about it! Certainly it is best always to use **Sie** if you are not sure about what to do, but it has to be said that negotiating the tricky social minefield from **Sie** to **du** is well worth the trouble.

There are a number of ways that a German might signal to you that he or she wants to become more friendly. The first is, quite simply, that your companion might suddenly switch. One second you hear '**Was machen Sie heute Abend?**' ('What are you going to do this evening?' i.e. **Sie** form), and the next you hear '**Möchtest du mit uns ins Kino kommen?**' ('Would you like to come with us to the cinema?' i.e. **du** form). Once this happens, it is appropriate for you to respond with **du**.

Another signal is when a German rather formally tells you his or her first name. You might have just said 'Herr Altdorfer', and your companion responds with something like '**Ich heiß' doch Micha**' (equivalent to 'Come on, call me Micha'). You would be expected to respond by giving your own first name, and you might even shake hands, to seal the new friendship.

One last method to establish the new mode of address is to use the phrase '**Wollen wir uns duzen?**' ('Shall we use **du** with each other?'), the appropriate response being something like '**schön**' (lovely) or '**klar doch**' (but of course).

As mentioned earlier, don't panic about this particular custom in Germany: if in doubt, you cannot go wrong by addressing everybody you meet with the formal **Sie**. If it's any consolation, the transitional period can be quite problematic even for the natives, so there is no need to let it bother you unduly – Germans usually make allowances for foreigners anyway. But when a German does offer you the **du** form be aware that they are offering the first step of what could become a beautiful friendship – Germans take their relationships with **du** friends very seriously and value such relationships highly.

Women in Germany

You will certainly have noticed that many of the chapters dealing with Germany's history, literature, and so on have featured only very few women. Up until the second half of the 20th century Germany was a male-dominated society, almost to the exclusion of women in public life. Although women have had the vote in Germany since 1918, until the 1970s, for instance, they still had very few rights in a marriage. Until this time, too, a law insisted that a woman was responsible for looking after house and family, and could only take a job with her husband's permission! Of course, many couples had ignored this, and other extremely sexist laws, for many years before, but the fact that it was still in force is indicative of the problems faced by women in Germany.

Interestingly, in the area of equality of the sexes, the East German regime was actually way ahead of its West German neighbour. Whether out of economic necessity or otherwise, women were actively encouraged to go out to work, and childcare was provided for every working family. This is just one area which many eastern Germans claim they miss about the old system, much to the annoyance of many western Germans!

Women's movement

Before there was any kind of formal women's movement in Germany, the two world wars had done much to further their cause, as in other industrial countries. Not only did women play a vital role on the home front during the war, but they were largely responsible for keeping the countries going in the years immediately after the war. Indeed, the huge losses incurred by the Germans meant that there was a huge surplus of women in society, even when all the German POWs returned home. This was bound to have an effect on the role of women in general.

One of the major figures to promote women's equality in the 1970s was an American/German woman called Petra Kelly. She was one of the founding members of **Die Grünen** (the Green Party, see Chapter 8) and linked her campaigning for women's rights firmly with her beliefs in environmental reform. Her gentle but passionate style of public speaking did much to advance her cause, and she was a very popular political figure until she withdrew from party politics in the 1980s. Although it is difficult to attribute the founding of a German **Frauenbewegung** (women's movement) to her, she did more than virtually any other individual to bring women into more prominence in public life.

Women in work

In this area, too, (West) Germany was rather slow in providing support for women who wanted to have families but continue working. **Kindergeld** (child benefit) was only introduced in 1986, and is a monthly sum of several hundred marks paid for the first year after a child is born. At the same time women were granted the right to **Mutterschaftsurlaub** (maternity leave) from their work, with normal pay and pension rights, and the guarantee that they will be able to return to their posts at the end of their leave.

Despite these improvements, women are still disadvantaged in the workplace. Although over one-third of Germany's workforce is female, statistics show that they are still paid relatively less for the same jobs, and that promotion tends to be harder to come by. Even **Beamtenstellen** (civil servant posts, including teachers in Germany), who are at least paid the same, are dominated by men in the senior positions.

Women in the armed forces

One interesting area of (in)equality in Germany is the **Bundeswehr** (armed forces). Germany still has **Wehrdienst** (compulsory military service) for all men over 18, but not for women. For a while, it was argued that women should be called up for military service like men, but the debate has now broadened to question the validity of **Wehrdienst** at all (more on this topic in the next chapter). Instead, the debate has now switched to look at the issue of equal rights for professional troops. Technically, the German **Grundgesetz** forbids women to bear arms, and so women in the armed forces are still only allowed to join as medical personnel or members of the musical corps. But in practice women receive exactly the same basic training, including weapons training, and more and more are finding themselves in the front line (largely as a result of Balkans peace-keeping duties). In 1999, a 22-year-old **Soldatin** (female soldier), Tanja Kreil, took the **Bundeswehr** to the European Court of Human Rights, claiming that she should be allowed to serve alongside men as a full soldier. In January 2000 the Court upheld Frau Kreil's complaint, paving the way, possibly, to women serving in all areas of the German armed forces in future.

Surnames and marriage

One outcome of the **Frauenbewegung** in Germany was that many women refused to give up their maiden names when they married. It is very common, therefore, to come across couples in Germany now with 'double-barrelled' names, such as Schmidt-Bauer or even for the man and woman to put their own surname first, and that of their partner second, so that you end up with Herr Schmidt-Bauer and Frau Bauer-Schmidt.

Another result of the move towards equality during the latter half of the 20th century is that a woman can now initiate divorce proceedings. Although not directly linked, this may have contributed to the steady increase in divorce in Germany, from 48,896 in 1946, to 187,802 in 1997.

The environment

If there is one subject close to the Germans' hearts nowadays, it is **die Umwelt** (the environment). Perhaps it is because their ancestors lived in the impenetrable germanic forests, but German people can be pretty fanatical about their environment: whether it be long, healthy walks in the woods, collecting their glass and paper for recycling, or campaigning against nuclear reprocessing plants, **die Umwelt** is a serious affair.

It all began, perhaps, with the 18th-century Romantics – people like Goethe and Caspar David Friedrich who wrote and painted subjects taken from the natural world, and linked nature with something essentially German. But the modern sense of 'green' awareness was first triggered by the natural disaster of the great forests dying because of acid rain in the 1980s. Almost as soon as the problem was identified a campaign swung into action to improve the environment. Germany has led the way in recycling, by introducing **der grüne Punkt** (green dot) on all recycleable packaging, has done much of the pioneering work on alternative power sources for lorries, buses and cars, and favours energy conservation at work and in the home – all done according to the slogan '**der Umwelt zuliebe**' ('for the sake of the environment'). Do not be surprised, when in Germany, if you get approving looks when you throw a glass bottle into a rubbish container, if you climb onto a natural gas-powered bus in a citycentre, or if you are forced to drive at under 100km/h on the **Autobahn** when there is a smog/ozone alert. ... As we have already said, the country which was the first in the world to elect a Green Party MP to its parliament (in 1983) and which now has the **Bündnis 90 / Die Grünen** sharing power with the SPD, takes its environmental responsibilities very seriously. Some might even say that it is the new religion in Germany. In a recent survey of 15- to 25-year-old Germans, which asked the question 'What issues are worth fighting for / against?' a staggering 95 per cent of the interviewees considered the top priority to be 'the environment'. 'Social injustice' was the second highest issue, albeit with a very respectable 90 per cent!

Religious observance

The origins of the first German **Reich** lay in the Catholic church, and Martin Luther was instrumental in establishing the Protestant church; as a result, Germany is today still divided along religious lines between those areas which have remained true to Rome, and those which embraced the 'new' Christian religion. As a rough guide, the north, east and central regions of Germany tend to be Protestant, while the south and the west are, on the whole, Protestant. Many people even feel that these faiths have influenced the way that the different parts of Germany have developed, and it is hard to dispute this: people and lifestyles in the north are considered conscientious, plain, upstanding and hardworking, while the south is seen as more flamboyant, open, warmhearted and fun-loving.

Nowadays, however, there is no obligation for individuals to be practising Christians. Indeed, a survey of 1995 revealed that over 25 million Germans would describe themselves as 'not religious' (31 per cent of the population). Only about 15 per cent claimed to be regular churchgoers, but the vast majority would still happily write either **katholisch** (Catholic, 33.9 per cent) or **evangelisch** (Protestant, 35.0 per cent) if a form asked them to state their **Konfession**. Many also continue to pay their **Kirchensteuer** (church tax), a voluntary 1 per cent tax deduction which is donated to the denomination of their choice, although this custom is also in decline.

For many people, the Church lost its credibility in the Nazi period when it threw its lot in with Hitler, despite the protests of a very few individual clergymen like Martin Niemöller and Dietrich Bonhoeffer, who died in concentration camps for their opposition to the regime. Some of this credibility was restored by the actions of the Protestant church in the Democratic Republic, from where opposition groups coordinated their demonstrations against the regime in the autumn of 1989.

As far as other Christian denominations are concerned, they have made very few inroads against the dominance of the two mainstream churches. Non-conformism never really challenged the Protestant church, although there are Baptist, Methodist and Evangelical churches in many cities. Significantly, most Germans would dismiss all these churches as **Sekten**, and know little about non-conformism.

Judaism in Germany

It might come as something of a surprise to learn that there is still a Jewish presence in Germany, considering the events of 1933–1945. But the fact is that many Jews consider themselves Jewish and German in equal measure, and many therefore chose to return to Germany after the war. Synagogues were rebuilt, contacts with the non-Jewish German community re-established, and an attempt was made to return to normality. But the fact remains that so many German Jews died in the Nazi period that a large proportion of the survivors did not want to return.

Relations between the Jewish community and German authorities have been a little strained in recent times for two reasons. The first is the ongoing battle for compensation for concentration-camp survivors. Although huge sums have been paid to Germany's neighbours over the years, relatively little compensation has been paid to German Jews. Many were forced by the Nazis to work for German firms and industrial centres, and were often literally worked to death. The fact that several of the firms involved are still trading in Germany has enraged the Jews (and a great many non-Jewish Germans, it must be said). They are particularly keen to get compensation as this generation is now in old age, and more and more are dying without seeing justice. It is a common sight nowadays to see people dressed as concentration camp inmates (their distinctive grey and white striped suits and yellow stars are still a highly emotive image in Germany) protesting outside shareholders' meetings and AGMs. In 1999, shareholders of **IG Farben**, the chemical company which developed the notorious Cyclon B chemical for the Nazis, voted to release profits to the affected Jews, but details of the sums involved have not yet been agreed.

The other big issue has been over the planned **Holocaust-Denkmal** (holocaust memorial) in Berlin, which has turned into one of the biggest public debates in Germany in recent years, eclipsing at times even the controversy over the government's move to Berlin. Of course, opinions have differed over what form the memorial should take, but for a long time the Jewish community felt slighted by the fact that they were not even consulted as to their opinions.

Racism

Despite the advances made in German-Jewish relations over the preceding years, the fear of neo-Nazism is still very strong. This is nowhere better seen than in the public response to overt acts of racism in Germany. Although the **Fünfprozentklausel** (5 per cent clause – see Chapter 8) and the **Grundgesetz** have together managed to curb the rise of any official neo-Nazi parties in politics, extreme right groups have enjoyed a small but significant success over the years. This has been especially the case in regions with high unemployment, and it is then quite common to see '**Ausländer raus**' ('Foreigners out') sprayed on walls.

Acts of racism in Germany have ranged from unfavourable treatment in government offices, or verbal abuse, to desecration of Jewish cemeteries and arson attacks on homes for asylum seekers, some of which have resulted in the deaths of inhabitants of these homes. Although much of what occurs is no different from the acts of extremists in every country, the issue is, quite rightly, considered to have far greater significance in Germany. Expensive TV and advertising campaigns have run in recent years, with, for example, top football stars stating emphatically, '**Auch Ausländer sind meine Freunde**' ('Foreigners are my friends too').

The 'typical' German

So is there such a thing as a typical German? Probably not, any more than we could agree on the characteristics of the typical Englishman, Australian, Frenchman or Chinese. What we can say, however, is that a German is likely to be unfailingly polite, a devoted friend when you start to **duzen**, interested in politics and green issues, a hard worker and someone with a great sense of humour, which you will certainly come to share if you make the effort to understand what 'makes him tick'. And yes, he probably does drink an awful lot of beer ... enjoy it!

GLOSSARY

der Stereotyp *stereotype*
ein Sinn (m.) **für Humor** *sense of humour*
die Preußen *the Prussians*
das deutsche Volk *the German race/people*
die Bevölkerung (-en) *population*
die Minoritäten / die Minderheiten *the minorities*

der Ausländer (-) / die Ausländerin (-nen) *foreigner*
der Judaismus *Judaism*
der Rassismus *racism*
die Umwelt *environment*
recyceln *to recycle*
die Kirche (-n) *the Church*
die Gemeinde (-n) *congregation, parish, church community*

Taking it further

If you cannot manage a trip to Germany just yet, but would like to observe the German people, try to watch as many contemporary German films as possible, either on TV or from your local video store. Although the cinema can sometimes distort the image it portrays of a particular race, it is usually a pretty true reflection of their habits and concerns. See Chapter 7 again for a list of recommended films.

One useful website is that of the **Bundesamt für Statistik** (Federal Office of Statistics), which publishes census information and reports on current trends etc. You will find it at www.statistik-bund.de.

12 | INTO THE FUTURE – GERMANY IN THE WIDER WORLD

For many observers a new era in German history dawned on 9 November 1989 when East and West Berliners scrambled onto the Wall and in one fell swoop brought the Cold War to an end. Gradually, as the years followed reunification, it became apparent that there were still some pretty tough mountains to climb before Germany could properly shake off the legacy of both Hitler's dreadful reign and the ideological stand-off of the Cold War. For although the country was, on the surface at least, united at last, it was clear that many of the tensions which had been inherited from the Nazi period, and continued under the Socialist rule, had not been properly examined, and laid to rest. The phrase **Vergangenheitsbewältigung**, 'coming to terms with Germany's Nazi legacy', now had to be expanded to include the problems of the Cold War.

German identity: German? European? Weltbürger?

It all boils down to the question 'What does *German* mean?' Much of what we have discussed in this book answers that question for an outsider, but does little to explain the German's own sense of identity.

Two key events in Germany's 20th century history influence the way a German feels about his or her identity. By now you might well have realised that these events are the Nazi rule of 1933–1945 and the existence of an East German state (1949–1989). Both, in different ways, shattered the ultra-confident sense of nationalism built up throughout the 19th century, culminating in Bismarck's triumphant unification of the all-powerful central European state in 1871.

The Second World War

The period after the fall of Hitler's regime was traumatic for the German nation, to say the least. After the heady days of the 1930s and early 1940s, people woke up in May 1945 to the grim reality that they had been living under an odious dictatorship. The victorious Allies forced all Germans to undergo a programme of 'denazification', of which compulsory visits to the concentration camps was only a small part. In all aspects of public life individuals and groups tried to make sense of what they had done, and lived through. Literature, politics, education and even, say, industrial relations in the post-war period were influenced by the process which came to be known as **Vergangenheitsbewältigung** (coming to terms with the past). In both the Soviet and western zones of occupation the Allies purged public bodies and political institutions of any personnel with direct connections to the Nazis and, to all intents and purposes, society was gradually ridded of its tarnished façade.

But none of these measures worked as well as might have been expected. Deep down, German society knew that it was guilty by association, and looked for a more telling way to sever its connections with the past. In the West, at least, this resolved itself in a kind of mass denial of German identity. Although American culture had been popular before the Nazis came to power, in the late-1940s it came to dominate: Coca-Cola, rock music and bubble gum came to be associated with everything that was wholesome and progressive, and with it came the virtual obsession with the English language which is so characteristic of the Germans nowadays. Ever since that time, then, most Germans – particularly of the younger generations – would say that they were **Weltbürger** (citizens of the world) first, and German last ... if at all.

The Democratic Republic

The situation is a little more complex for Germans who found themselves living in the eastern half of Germany after the war. Within a few years they were part of a new regime, allied to the Soviets, which certainly seemed intent on cleansing Germany of its Nazi associations. It has since been recognised that the East German authorities were far more successful in purging public life of ex-Nazis, unlike the West, where they often re-entered politics after just a few years, if they had been forced to leave at all. Many East German citizens genuinely felt that their brand of Socialism was the way forward, and looked to the future with cautious optimism.

But in the ideological battle of the Cold War it all went horribly wrong. While the citizens of the East were far happier to call themselves German in this period, it was apparent that all was not well in their state. As more and more people chose to leave for the West, the construction of the Wall in 1961 (a move designed to protect East German citizens from the pernicious influence of the West, and to prevent the 'brain drain' of educated workers), dismayed those left behind. Intellectuals who protested against the authorities were imprisoned, or expelled, and the notorious **Stasi** (the **Staatssicherheitsdienst** or State Security Service) recruited more and more ordinary people to spy upon their fellows. It was clear that East Germany had replaced one totalitarian regime with another.

That is not to say that life in the East was miserable, because there were aspects of the Socialist state which are missed even today, a decade after its decline. But here, too, Germans are faced with a new form of **Vergangenheitsbewältigung**. Each time a prominent East German author, actor or academic is revealed to have been an

inoffizieller Mitarbeiter (IM – unofficial informant) for the **Stasi**, recruited to give regular reports about the morale and political reliability of their friends and colleagues, the wounds are opened again.

Post-unification

The closest that many Germans came to feeling proud to be German in the 1960s to 1980s was in the sporting achievements of their respective states, and it is no coincidence that the two Germanies came to dominate in sports as varied as tennis, football and athletics. Here, finally, was a chance to applaud something German, to be able to say that you were proud to be German, if only for the 90 minutes of a soccer match. This sense of sporting pride has not disappeared in the post-**Wende** period, and indeed it is in the field of sport that eastern and western Germany have most successfully integrated. Yet even today, not many people, including sports fans, would claim to be proud to be German. Instead it is to Europe that many of them look for a sense of identity. More so than any other European nation, the Germans invest a great deal of their energies in Europe: turnout for Euro elections, for instance, is generally much higher than elsewhere. It is only through Europe, perhaps, that Germans can begin to feel proud of their own identity, safe in the knowledge that a Germany firmly embedded within a united Europe will never again be able to threaten European stability. So while most ordinary Germans regret the passing of the Mark, symbol of their miraculous recovery in the early post-war years, they see it as a necessary part of the integration process. More than any others, then, a German today is likely to see him or herself as a citizen of Europe. Ironically, though, it is this very process which looks set to return Germany to the centre of the political stage in Europe, achieving the very domination which Hitler's Panzer brigades could not.

German economic strength into the 21st century

Germany's financial strength has been a key part of the European process for many years now, and Germany was one of the most vocal supporters of the exchange mechanism of the mid-1990s, and the introduction of the Euro as a common European currency in 1999. The German **Bundesbank** (Federal Bank) in Frankfurt am Main has, while fiercely protecting its independence from the German government, nevertheless been instrumental in bringing about the conditions necessary for this next step in the process of European integration. At the same time, major German companies which had seen enormous financial growth throughout the 1970s and 1980s were able to sustain that growth after the collapse of the eastern European nations by acquiring part or all of the ailing nationalised industries in Poland, Hungary, the Czech Republic and so on. Volkswagen is a prime example of a highly successful domestic firm which had traditionally been a home producer, exporting around the world, which suddenly underwent massive expansion. In a few short years Volkswagen had interests in virtually every eastern European car manufacturer, and wholly owned Škoda, the Czech Republic's prize industry. In the late 1990s, those same industries were changing tactics again, adopting the Anglo-Saxon concept of competitive acquisition and large global corporations. By doing this they broadened their responsibilities, this time beyond the relatively limited horizons of their German shareholders' interests. It remains to be seen how successful these companies are in the world markets, but their actions are creating a new image of Germany abroad which can only serve to strengthen the country's standing.

Foreign policy today

One final consideration of current German standing within the European community and the wider world is the role that German forces have come to play in United Nations and NATO peace-keeping missions in the mid- to late 1990s. Here, perhaps more than anywhere else, is a sign of the rehabilitation of the German nation since the shame of Nazism.

Although both German states were quickly allowed into their respective military alliances after the war – West Germany was allowed to rearm and join NATO as early as 1955 – this was very much part of the Cold War stand-off between East and West and was not seriously meant to grant Germany any autonomy. Indeed, the two superpowers were planning any future conflict to take place in Germany, which would certainly have devastated the country. Added to this was the decidedly awkward situation faced by German soldiers, who knew that they would in all likelihood be fighting their own countrymen. However much they were prepared to do this, to defend the interests of their own ideology, it cannot have done much to boost Germany's damaged sense of identity in the 40 years of separation.

In terms of influence overseas, too, this situation was less than ideal for Germany. The West German armed forces, known as the **Bundeswehr**, were forbidden by the **Grundgesetz** to take part in military operations beyond Germany's own borders, and their training was entirely defensive in nature.

Once reunification took place, and the Cold War ended, however, the newly enlarged **Bundeswehr** was looking for a new role. The **Bundeswehr** was (and still is) an army built upon the principles of national service – **Wehrdienst** – for all males aged 18+. Although the terms and length of service have changed over the years, generally getting shorter as time has gone by, the notion of the **Bürger in Uniform** (citizen in uniform) has been championed as an important safeguard against another Nazi state, where the army kept itself apart from its people.

Gulf War

When the Gulf War broke out in 1991, then Defence Minister Klaus Kinkel pledged **Bundeswehr** support for the Allied war against Saddam Hussein in Kuwait and Iraq. He immediately ran into trouble with his country's constitution, however, and in the end Germany's contribution amounted to the deployment of a number of airborne early warning aircraft and missile defence batteries in Turkey, still within NATO territory.

Even then, he was faced with the embarrassing protests of national servicemen in the missile units, who claimed that they were being sent overseas illegally. They were brought home and replaced with professional troops, but the outcry in public and political circles showed that any greater involvement in world affairs would have to be handled very carefully indeed. For a number of years following this conflict, Germany sent medics to troublespots around the world, notably Somalia, on United Nations missions, but the issue of armed conflict overseas seemed to have passed.

The Balkans

A key event in the gradual rehabilitation of Germany as a world state came with the Balkans crisis in late 1991. As conditions in Sarajevo and Bosnia deteriorated, it was Germany who took the bold step of recognising the claims of Bosnia, Croatia and Slovenia to sovereign status. Although many other European and United Nations countries were annoyed by Germany's unilateral action, it did trigger off a gradual improvement for the people suffering in those countries: under the terms of the Dayton Peace Treaty in 1995, UN-controlled troops were sent to Sarajevo and the surrounding region as peace-keeping troops. Much more significant, however, was that German troops were involved in this operation. For the first time in over 40 years, German soldiers, equipped with weapons and light tanks, were deployed into another European country ... and one which Hitler's troops had invaded during the Second World War. Despite concerns within Germany, and Europe, the German soldiers performed admirably under the spotlight of the world's press, clearing mines, building bridges and undertaking reconnaissance patrols of their designated areas. At the same time, the **Bundesmarine** (Federal German Navy) was taking part in the maritime embargo in the Adriatic Sea, contributing to the world's efforts to prevent arms and ammunition reaching Yugoslavia, and the **Luftwaffe** (Air Force) flew combat patrols in the skies of Bosnia from airbases in Italy.

The participation of the German troops in this peace-keeping action required parliamentary consent, which was granted, after fierce debate, in April 1993. It was then ratified by the **Bundesver-fassungsgericht** the following year. This was a huge step for Germany, enabling the **Bundeswehr** to take up a place within NATO as an equal partner, and allowing Germany to enjoy an enhanced reputation within the United Nations. But it was a first step, with more to come from the Balkans within a few years.

In 1999, the melting pot of the Balkans began to boil over again, this time in the Yugoslavian province of Kosovo. Here, the Serbian

authorities seemed to be tolerating, or, even worse, promoting a civil war which pitched the dominant Serb population against the numerically superior ethnic Albanian population. It was a conflict which has been going on in this region for centuries, but as pictures of the Kosovo Albanians' miseries were beamed to the rest of the world, popular sentiment demanded that the world community act to prevent the 'ethnic cleansing'. Although the United Nations declined to intervene, the countries of NATO acted with a concerted campaign of air attacks against Serbia, both inside Kosovo and in the country at large. In what was seen as an historic action, units of the **Bundeswehr** flew alongside aircraft of the British RAF, the American USAF and other NATO air forces, in aggressive flights to destroy key Serbian army bases, but also important bridges, factories and power plants.

The response to this action was mixed: in Britain, the *Sun* newspaper published a leading article approving of Germany's participation as a paid-up NATO member. They printed a cartoon of Second World War RAF and **Luftwaffe** pilots looking down on their present-day successors with approval. But in Germany, things were less clear. Not only were large numbers of ordinary Germans unsure of the **Luftwaffe**'s participation (especially when the air campaign seemed, initially, to result in worse atrocities against the Kosovo Albanians, who now flooded across the Albanian border, threatening an escalation of the war), but the **Bundestag** was bitterly divided. In long and often heated debates, MPs compared the Serbs' policy of ethnic cleansing with the Holocaust and argued that Germany, of all countries, was morally obliged to prevent it.

Others, by way of contrast, stressed that the post-war German state could never again be allowed to take part in a war of aggression. Nowhere was the dilemma better illustrated than within the ranks of the Green Party, which was quickly learning the difficult lessons of life in power. While Chancellor Schröder's SPD were largely behind the military operation, the Greens were split between the '**Fundis**' (fundamentalists), who argued the pacifist line, and the '**Realos**' (realists), who accepted the action – and Germany's participation – as necessary.

At the Green Party's conference, which coincided with the height of the air campaign in June 1999, it seemed as if the whole German position was represented. The Green leader, Joska Fischer, was booed and heckled by his own members as he pleaded with party members to support Germany's contribution to the NATO operation. For a few days it looked like he might lose control of his party, which in turn could have led to a collapse of the German SPD/Green government. In the end, Fischer kept control – just – and the Green Party agreed to support the war, but it had been a close run thing.

In the end, there was never a need for ground troops to fight their way into Kosovo, but German troops were ready to march with their NATO allies. When the NATO peace-keeping troops entered Kosovo after Serbia's withdrawal, the **Bundeswehr** played an important role in policing their allocated area, and Germany took up its new position within the world community as a full member of the USA and NATO's self-allocated role as world policemen. At the time of writing, German troops were still deployed in both Bosnia and Kosovo: in many ways, the **Bundesrepublik Deutschland** has come of age as a political power within Europe, more than 50 years after the collapse of Hitler's **Reich**.

Into the future

It is still too early to draw concrete conclusions about where Germany will go next. The current SPD administration still faces huge problems with its overhaul of the welfare state; the press still worries about the low birthrate of Germans; environmental problems still plague large areas of German forest; and German troops are still mounting armed patrols in Bosnia and Kosovo. But one thing is sure: the nation which emerged, phoenix-like, from the ashes of the shattered Nazi state has been a huge success in democracy. In a speech on 7 September 1999 marking the 50th anniversary of the founding of the **Bundesrepublik**, the President of the **Bundestag**, Wolfgang Thierse, summed up Germany's post-war history with two words: '**Wohlstand und Frieden**' (prosperity and peace). Despite the many problems which still trouble this young democracy, the majority of observers would predict continued '**Wohlstand und Frieden**' in the years to come.

GLOSSARY

die Nachkriegszeit *the post-war period*

der Weltbürger (-), die Weltbürgerin (-nen) *world citizen*

die Bundeswehr *German Federal Armed Forces*

der Golfkrieg *the Gulf War*

die Vereinten Nationen (die UNO) *the United Nations* (the UN)

die Friedenstruppen *peace-keeping forces*

den Frieden erhalten *to preserve/protect the peace*

einsetzen / im Einsatz sein *to deploy / to be on deployment, on a mission*

die Politik *politics*

Taking it further

The contemporary nature of the events outlined in this chapter means that it is difficult to recommend any books which deal specifically with Germany's current foreign policy: this is where the press and the Internet come into their own.

If you receive German television via satellite or cable, and you can follow German TV (don't worry if you don't understand all that much of the German, you will be surprised how the pictures help to give you an idea of the story), try watching the channel **n-tv**. This is a 24-hour news channel with regular bulletins throughout the day, and live broadcasts of important parliamentary debates etc.

Another good source of up-to-date information is the Internet: try logging onto one of the big search engines, like www.yahoo.de or www.web.de for a news 'ticker', or alternatively you can browse the Federal Government's web sites (see Chapter 8).

Finally, any of the good current affairs magazines in Germany, or the English language publications *Time*, *Newsweek* or the *Financial Times*, publish regular features about developments in Germany.

Appendix A: Timeline of Historical and

Key to symbols:
📖 Literary movement   🖼 Artistic movement
♪ Musical movement   🏛 Architectural style
☺ Philosophical/Political movement

Historical events

Before Christ

50,000 BC	First known Europeans settle in Neander Valley (*Neanderthal*) near Düsseldorf

1st century AD – 5th century AD

9 AD	Roman force defeated in the Teutoburger Wald by German leader Hermann (Arminius)
ca. **300**	Germanic clans beginning to form larger tribes: Huns, Saxons, Goths, Vandals, etc.
451	Attila the Hun; barbarians start to invade Roman Germany
486	Frankish King Clovis establishes first great German dynasty

6th century – 10th century

718	St Boniface spreads Christianity throughout German tribes
743	Pepin founds dynasty later known as Carolingian
800	Charlemagne (d. 814) crowned emperor of Holy Roman Empire
843	Treaty of Verdun effectively divides Charlemagne's empire into West Frankland (France) and the German Frankish lands
911	Kingdom of Germany formed by Henry of Saxony
936	Henry's son, Otto the Great, crowned Emperor
955	Otto's united German army defeats Hungarians at Lechfeld

Cultural Events in Germany

Cultural events	Events of global significance
Imperial Baths & Porta Nigra, Trier	*c.* **30** Christ crucified
Limes frontier	**117** Roman Empire reaches zenith
Bishop Wulfila's Gothic Bible	**334** Alexander the Great
	730 1st printing in China
🏛 Carolingian	
c. **750** *Hildebrandslied*	
Fulda Abbey	
🏛 Ottonian	
Magdeburg Cathedral	

Historical events

11th century

1002   Death of Otto III. His successor, Henry II, withdraws from
           Roman politics and concentrates on building up Germany
1024   Conrad II begins the Salian dynasty. Years of struggle between
           German Emperors and Roman Popes ensue

12th century

1152   Friedrich I (Barbarossa) ascends the throne - Hohenstaufen
           dynasty

13th century

1226   Knights of Teutonic Order begin crusade to convert the Slavs
           to the east – the state of Prussia is established

14th century

1358   Hanseatic League of trading cities founded

15th century

1493   Maximilian I crowned Emperor of 'Holy Roman Empire of the
           German Nation'

Cultural events	**Events of global significance**
🏛 Romanesque	*c.* **1000** Vikings reach America
1039 Cathedral at Speyer completed	
	1066 Norman invasion of Britain
	1095 1st crusades
1098 Birth of Hildegard of Bingen, one of the greatest composers of medieval music in Europe	
📖 Minnesang & Epic Storytelling	
1170 Probable birth of Walther von der Vogelweide	
1200 The *Nibelungenlied* is written	
	1206 Ghengis Khan begins conquest of Asia
🏛 Gothic	
	1244 Jerusalem taken by Muslims
1248 Construction of Cologne Cathedral begins (completed 1880)	
1337 100 Years War between Britain & France	
1348 Black Death ravages Europe	
🖼 ☺ Renaissance	
1445 Gutenberg print 1st book in Europe	
1471 Birth of Albrecht Dürer (d. 1528) 1st religious carvings by e.g. Tilman Riemenschneider	
	1492 Columbus reaches America

Historical events

16th century

1517	Luther sparks Reformation
1531	League of Schmalkalden to protect Protestant states
1555	Peace of Augsburg guarantees religious freedoms

17th century

1618	Defenestration of Prague, 30 Years War (>1648)
1648	Peace of Westphalia ends 30 Years War

18th century

1701	Friedrich I begins Prussian expansionism
1740	Succession of Friedrich II 'der Große' (d. 1786)
1756	Seven Years War - Prussia grows in strength

Cultural events	Events of global significance
🏛 ♪ ☺ Reformation & Counter-Reformation	**1543** Copernicus proposes that the Earth revolves around the sun
	1620 Mayflower Pilgrims land in America
1627 Schütz, *Dafne* - 1st German opera **1650** First daily newspaper appears in Leipzig **1669** Grimmelshausen, *Der abentheuerlicher Simplicissimus Teutsch* – first successful German novel	**1666** Newton's Theory of Gravity
☺ 🏚 Age of Enlightenment 🏛 ♪ Baroque & Rococo **1711** Construction of Dresden *Zwinger* **1721** Bach's Brandenburg concertos	
🏚 Sturm und Drang **1782** Schiller, *Die Räuber* 🏛 Neo-Classicism **1791** Brandenburg Gate **1791** Mozart, *Die Zauberflöte*	**1769** Cook reaches Australia **1769** Watt's steam engine heralds Industrial Revolution **1776** US Declaration of Independence **1789** French Revolution

Historical events

19th century

1806	Confederation of the Rhine
	14.10 Battles of Jena & Auerstadt. Napoleon defeats Prussia
1813	*Völkerschlacht* at Leipzig
1815	Allied Treaty of Vienna allows Germany a new Confederation
1834	Founding of *Deutscher Zollverein* sees the Prussian *Thaler* become common German currency. Austria ostracized
1848	Parliament assembled at Frankfurt
1862	Bismarck appointed *Ministerpresident* of Prussia
1866	Austro-Prussian war
1870	Franco-Prussian war
1871	18.01 Kaiser Wilhelm I proclaimed Emperor of II. Reich Germany united
1890	Bismarck forced to resign

Cultural events	Events of global significance
1772–1825 Goethe's *Faust*	
🖾 ♪ 📖 Romantic	
	1815 Napoleon defeated at Waterloo
1818 C. D. Friedrich's painting *Wanderer über dem Nebelmeer*	**1822** 1st photographs
1823 Beethoven's 9th Symphony	
1835 First steam locomotive in Germany travels from Nuremberg to Fürth	
1836 Büchner, *Woyzeck*	
☺ Marx & Engels, *Communist Manifesto*	Revolution in France
	1854 Japan opens its borders to USA trade
	1861 American Civil War
1876 Wagner, *Ring des Nibelungen*	
🏛 🖾 📖 *Jugendstil* (art nouveau)	
	1885 Daimler & Benz build prototype automobiles
1886 Nietzsche, *Jenseits von Gut und Böse*	
📖 *Bürgerlicher Realismus*	
1888 Storm's *Novelle*, *Der Schimmelreiter*	
	1895 Röntgen develops x-rays
1895 1st public film performances	

Historical events

1st half of 20th century

1914	28.06 Assassination of Archduke Ferdinand triggers World War I (>11.11.1918)
1918 >	Series of Governments struggle in Weimar Republic
1919	Treaty of Versailles imposes harsh conditions on Germany
1923	Hitler writes *Mein Kampf* in jail after failed *putsch*
1933	30.01 Hitler becomes Chancellor
1938	*Anschluß* of Austria - Nazi expansion unchecked
1939	1.09 Poland invaded. World War II (>8.05.1945)
1944	6.06 Allied invasion of mainland Europe on D-Day
1945	8.05 Unconditional German surrender
	Germany divided between USA, GB & France, and Soviet Union

Post-world war two

1949	Foundation of *BRD* (23.05) & *DDR* (7.10)
	Wirtschaftswunder
1953	Uprising in East Berlin put down
1955	*BRD* enters NATO
1961	13.08 Berlin Wall
1969	*Ostpolitik – détente* between *BRD* & *DDR*
1989	9.11 Fall of Berlin Wall
1990	3.10 Reunification of Germany

Cultural events	Events of global significance
🎭 📖 Expressionism	
1901 Mann, *Buddenbrooks*	**1903** Wright brothers' 1st flight
1905 *Die Brücke* art group	
1905 Einstein's Theory of Relativity	
1911 *Der blaue Reiter* art	
Kafka, *Der Prozeß*	**1913** Henry Ford begins mass-production of cars
	1917 Russian Revolution
🏛 **1919** Bauhaus school founded	
1929 Remarque, *Im Westen nichts Neues*	**1929** Wall Street crash - global recession
	1934 Chinese Communist 'Long March'
	1936 Spanish Civil War
	United Nations founded
☺ *Stunde Null*	Cold War
📖 *Vergangenheitsbewältigung*	
1947 *Gruppe 47* founded	**1948** State of Israel founded
1951 Böll, *Wo warst du, Adam?*	
1959 Grass, *Blechtrommel*	
1963 Wolf, *Der geteilte Himmel* - GDR fiction	**1969** Moon landing
	1992 Break-up of Soviet Union
1998 Reforms of German language	

APPENDIX B: SOME TYPICAL GERMAN CUISINE

Back in Chapter 6 we discussed some typical German dishes. In the following few pages of this appendix you will find one or two examples of recipes which will allow you to recreate some of the tastes of Germany. In each case you will find the recipe first of all in German, just like you might find it written out in someone's recipe book in Düsseldorf, Stuttgart or Dresden. If you are feeling really adventurous, you could try preparing the dish solely from these German notes. If, however, you don't trust yourself to get it right, we have prepared an English translation so that you can still have a go. The recipes we have chosen are as follows

Sauerbraten 'Rheinischer Art' – Rheinland Sour Roast Beef

This is a dish which you might find in many of the towns along the Rhine valley, and is unusual because it is based on beef, which is not the commonest meat in German cuisine by any stretch of the imagination. Note that one of the ingredients is **Speck**, which can be translated either as 'bacon', or as 'ham', but is not really either. It is a smoked pork which generally comes in thick slices, and is used in cubes in many dishes.

Weihnachtsstollen – Christmas 'Stollen' cake

A traditional Christmas serving which can be found anywhere in Germany. It is quite a heavy dough cake, which is often served in slices, and liberally smeared in butter. One ingredient which you may not have heard of is **Quark**, which is a soft cream cheese. It can be found in many supermarkets outside Germany nowadays, generally alongside other 'exotic' cheeses like Italian mascarpone and mozzarella. Incidentally, if you buy more Quark than you need for this recipe, it makes a lovely base for a refreshing fresh fruit salad!

Kartoffelpuffer – Potato cakes

This is a favourite snack at open-air events in Germany wherever small stallholders are selling warm products (their booths are often called **Imbiss-Ständer**). It is served over the counter, wrapped in some paper, and often covered in a thick apple sauce. At Christmas markets you would probably enjoy your **Kartoffelpuffer** with a hot glass of **Glühwein** (mulled wine). Delicious!

Sauerbraten – Rheinische Art

Sauerbraten (Rheinische Art)

Beize:
3/4 l Wasser,
1/4 l Essig,
2 Lorbeerblätter,
2 Wachholderbeeren,
2 Nelken,
1 Teelöffel
   Pfefferkörner,
2 Zwiebeln in
   Ringen,
Suppengrün,
1 kg Rindfleisch,
(aus der Keule
   ohne Knochen)
Salz,
Pfeffer,
4 Esslöffel Öl
1 Tasse Wasser
100 g geräucherten
   Speck in
   Scheiben,
1/4 l Sahne,
1 Esslöffel Mehl
50 g gewaschene
   Rosinen
Beilagen:
Kartoffelknödel

Die Beize mit allen Zutaten aufkochen und erkalten lassen. Das Fleisch 2-3 Tage in die Beize legen, es muss von der Flüssigkeit ganz bedeckt sein. Mit einem sauberen Tuch abdecken. Das Fleisch aus der Beize nehmen, gut trocken tupfen, mit Salz und Pfeffer gut einreiben. Das Öl erhitzen, das Fleisch allseits gut anbräunen und in ein Bratgeschirr mit Deckel setzen. In das Bratgeschirr 1 Tasse mit Beize vermischtes Wasser, die Gewürze aus der Beize, Suppengrün und Zwiebeln geben. Das Fleisch mit Speckscheiben belegen. In den gut vorgeheizten Backofen schieben und bei Mittelhitze braten. Nach ca. 120 Minuten das Fleisch herausnehmen und warm stellen.

Den Bratenfond loskochen, alles durch ein Sieb streichen. Die Sahne mit dem Mehl glattrühren, der Soße zugeben, gut rühren, aufkochen und ggf. mit Beize und fertiger Bratensoße abschmecken. Die Rosinen in die Soße geben, kurz aufkochen.

Garzeit: ca. 120 Min.   Elektroherd: 200 °C

Rhein 'Sour' Roast Beef

Marinade ingredients
$3/4$ l water
$1/4$ l vinegar
2 bay leaves
2 juniper berries
2 cloves
1 tsp peppercorns

salt and pepper
1 kg boned leg of beef
2 onions cut into rings
4 desertspoons oil
1 cup water
100 g sliced smoked bacon
$1/4$ l cream
1 dessertspoon plain flour
beef stock
50 g washed raisins

Boil all the marinade ingredients and leave to cool. Marinate the meat for 2–3 days making sure that it is completely covered by the liquid. Cover with a clean cloth.

Take the meat out of the marinade, pat dry, and rub in salt and pepper. Heat oil, brown all sides of the meat, and put into a deep frying pan with a lid. Add to this 1 cup of marinade mixed with water, the seasonings from the marinade, stock and onion rings. Cover the meat with pieces of bacon. Put into a preheated oven at a medium heat. After about 2 hours take the meat out of the oven and keep warm.

Reduce the cooking juices and pass through a sieve. Blend the cream and flour until smooth, add to the strained juices and stir well. Bring to the boil, and if need be add more marinade to taste. Add the raisins to the sauce and briefly reboil.

Cooking time: about 2 hours
Oven temperature: 200°C, Gas mark 4

Weihnachtsstollen

Weihnachtsstollen

150g Margarine oder Butter,
150g Zucker,
2 Päckchen Vanillinzucker,
3 Eier,
100g Mandeln,
100g Orangeat,
50g Zitronat,
250g Quark,
600g Mehl,
1 Päckchen Backpulver,
125g Rosinen,
Margarine zum Einfetten.
Mehl zum Bestäuben.
Zum Bestreichen:
50g zerlassene Butter,
25g Puderzucker

Butter, Zucker und Vanillinzucker in einer Schüssel schaumig rühren. Eier nach und nach dazugeben.
Orangeat und Zitronat fein hacken und mit Orangen- und Zitronensaft in die Schüssel geben.
Mandeln und Quark unterkneten. Mehl und Backpulver mischen und ebenfalls unterkneten, so dass ein fester Teig entsteht.
Rosinen in einem Sieb unter heißem Wasser gründlich abbrausen. Abtropfen lassen, trockenreiben. In etwas Mehl wälzen und in den Teig kneten. Den Teig zu einem dicken Oval formen und 2/3 umschlagen, dass die Form eines Stollen entsteht.
Auf ein eingefettetes und mit Mehl bestäubten Backblech im vorgeheizten Ofen backen. Nach 50 Minuten mit Alufolie abdecken und fertigbacken. Noch warm mit zerlassener Butter bestreichen und mit Puderzucker bestreuen.

Backzeit: 70 Minuten
Elektroherd: 200 °C
Gasherd: Stufe 4

Christmas 'Stollen' cake

Ingredients

150g margarine or butter
150g sugar
2 packets of vanilla sugar
3 eggs
100g almonds
100g candied orange peel
50g candied lemon peel

250g quark
600g plain flour
1 packet baking powder
125g raisins
margarine to grease the tin
flour to dust the tin

Before serving

50g melted butter
25g icing sugar

Beat butter, sugar and vanilla sugar in a bowl until frothy. Add eggs. Chop orange and lemon peel finely and add with a little orange and lemon juice to the bowl. Mix almonds and Quark thoroughly. Mix flour and baking powder together and blend into Quark so that a firm dough is formed.

Rinse raisins in a sieve with hot water. Leave to drain and then rub dry. Knead dough in a little flour. Form dough into a thick oval shape and fold up 2/3 lengthways so that it takes the form of a tunnel. Place the dough on a greased baking sheet, dusted with flour, and bake in a preheated oven. After 50 minutes cover with baking foil and continue baking until ready. Spread with melted butter whilst still warm and dust with icing sugar before serving.

Cooking time: 1 hour 10 minutes
Oven temperature: 200°C, Gas mark 4

Kartoffelpuffer

Kartoffelpuffer (Reibekuchen)

1 kg Kartoffeln,
1 große Zwiebel,
1-2 Eier
5 Esslöffel
  feine Haferflocken,
Salz,
Pfeffer,
1 Prise Muskatnuss,
Fett zum Ausbacken

Die geschälten Kartoffeln reiben,
ebenso die Zwiebel. Entstehende
Flüssigkeit abgießen. Alle übrigen
Zutaten unter die geriebenen
Kartoffeln mengen.
Das Fett in einer Pfanne gut
erhitzen, den Teig mit einem
Esslöffel portionsweise in das
heiße Fett geben, glattstreichen
und beiderseits goldgelb ausbacken.
Je nach Belieben mit Apfelmus
oder dünnen Lachsscheiben
servieren.

Garzeit : ca. 20 Minuten

Potato Cakes

Ingredients

1kg potatoes
1 large onion
1–2 eggs
5 dessertspoons fine rolled oats
salt and pepper
pinch of nutmeg
fat for frying

Grate the peeled potatoes and then likewise the onions. Drain off any excess liquid. Add all other ingredients to the grated potato mixture.

Heat the fat in a frying pan until very hot, place dessertspoon size portions of mixture into the fat, flatten slightly and fry both sides until golden and cooked.

Serve with apple sauce or thinly sliced salmon.

Cooking time: about 20 minutes.

INDEX